Rosa Luxemburg

Rosa Luxemburg

A REAPPRAISAL

Lelio Basso

Translated by Douglas Parmée

PRAEGER

NEW YORK

Published in the United States of America in 1975
by Praeger Publishers, Inc.
111 Fourth Avenue, New York, N.Y. 10003

Copyright © 1967 by Editori Riuniti
Translation copyright © 1975 by André Deutsch Limited

Library of Congress Cataloging in Publication Data

Basso, Lelio.
  Rosa Luxemburg, a reappraisal.

  Includes index.
  1. Luxemburg, Rosa, 1870–1919.
HC273.L83B29   335.43'092'4   72–93288
ISBN 0–275–19790–5

Printed in Great Britain

Contents

Introduction

ROSA LUXEMBURG was certainly one of the most effective and creative of the exponents of Marxism which, according to Engel's well-known definition, is not a dogma but a guide to action; so it is only natural for her name to have been almost forgotten during the long period when Marxism was distorted into opportunism on the one hand and dogmatism on the other. So it is not irrelevant to quote some of the more important statements of prominent members of the labour movement concerning Rosa Luxemburg. The best known of these is from Lenin who wrote in 1922:

> But in spite of her mistakes she was – and remains for us – an eagle. And not only will the memory of her always remain precious to Communists all over the world but her biography and her *complete* works (the publication of which the German Communists are inordinately delaying, which can only be excused by the tremendous losses they are suffering in their severe struggle), will serve as a useful lesson in the training of many generations of Communists all over the world.[1]

This judgement echoes that of Karl Radek, at that time one of the most prominent of the leaders of the Bolsheviks, in the work of commemorating her:

> What Rosa Luxemburg represented and still represents for the proletariat of Germany and other countries does not belong to the past but will appear only in the future, when her collected writings have been thoroughly studied by large sections of Communists and when they have steeped themselves in the spirit of her works. This does not mean that we Communists need share her every opinion. Anton Pannekoek criticized her book on the accumulation of capital and I myself adopted a critical attitude towards the positive side of her *Junius* pamphlet but no one speaking on behalf of Communism and thinking in Communist terms, can put these works down without being convinced that in Rosa Luxemburg Communism lost its most profound theoretical thinker, that she is our guide from whom Communist workers will need to learn for decades to come.[2]

The statement that Rosa Luxemburg was the most profound Communist thinker need not surprise us, even though it was made during Lenin's lifetime by one of the leading members of his own party; fifteen years earlier, Franz Mehring, an expert on Marx and Marxism, had felt able to write in Kautsky's review, *Die Neue Zeit* – and Kautsky was regarded almost unanimously as the leading interpreter of Marxism – that Rosa Luxemburg was 'the greatest genius amongst the scientific heirs of Marx and Engels'.[3] A similar judgement is found in Lukacs' preface to his collection of articles published under the title *Geschichte und Klassenbewusstsein* in 1922, when he defined Rosa Luxemburg as 'the only disciple of Marx who had continued his life's work both in the analysis of economic facts and in the sphere of economic method' and stated that 'from this point of view she was concretely related to the present stage of social development'.[4]

But notwithstanding the fact that the most illustrious exponents of Marxist thought had emphasized their importance, Rosa Luxemburg's theoretical works, scattered as they were in numerous pamphlets and dispersed in hundreds of articles and speeches were hidden under a thick blanket of silence and were accessible to only the most persistent scholars. On the one hand the rightest Social Democrats, who only a few weeks after coming to power in Germany had connived at, if not instigated,[5] Rosa Luxemburg's assassination in order to rid themselves of their most dangerous adversary, obviously had no interest in seeing a new edition of her works which seemed to be nothing but accusations directed against social democratic policy; on the other hand Stalin's rigid dogmatism could not allow the dissemination of any thought as rich and living as that of Rosa Luxemburg, which was, so to speak, a call to battle against any attempt to force Marxism into rigid, soulless formulas. Barely one year after Lenin's death, the enlarged executive body of the Communist Internationale condemned some of her doctrines, and at the beginning of the thirties any reprint of her works on the part of the Communists had become impossible and her name could only be pronounced in condemnatory terms; in the end, people speak of the Luxemburg pox[6] Consequently, more than forty years after Lenin had announced the edition of her complete works and had himself started work on it, they are still unpublished; it is, however, true that the Communists have begun to reprint her works, and a complete bibliography recently appeared in Poland which will be of great help to every scholar and future editor.

For Rosa Luxemburg, the central problem round which her whole theoretical work and practical action revolve was that of the socialist revolution: 'How and why can we, in general, achieve the ultimate goal of all our efforts?'[7] This was, incidentally, the central problem for Marx,[8] too, as it should be for every socialist for whom socialism is not merely a subject for facile speeches at Sunday public meetings but a fundamental, moral and political choice that must be translated into action. Marx had made a decisive contribution to the correct formulation of the problem and its solution, but his followers had either misunderstood or betrayed the spirit of Marxism in practice, and Rosa Luxemburg's whole endeavour was directed towards rediscovering this spirit, both on the plane of method and analysis as well as that of action.

The revolutionary tradition that had predominated until Marx, was naturally the tradition of the great French Revolution, and Marx and Engels were themselves deeply imbued with it. But the French Revolution was an historical phenomenon so richly and powerfully creative that even today, almost two centuries later, historians have not succeeded in exhausting its essential aspects and in understanding the full strength of its inner dynamism. It is thus not surprising if its immediate successors seized on certain isolated aspects and reached false and one-sided conclusions, the more so as within the Revolution itself contradictory forces were at work which could not fail to give rise to strong emotional counter-currents. And so, the conservatives tended to criticize the Revolution and its ideals in the name of the laws and continuity of history, while the forces of the left tended to attack the results of the Revolution because they had failed to fulfil ideals that the Revolution had itself proclaimed. But the left itself was deeply divided as to the means of realizing these unfulfilled ideals, that is to say, of continuing the historical process. Accordingly, as the emphasis was placed on one or other of these aspects of the Revolution, there were on the one hand those who advocated constructing systems and, on the other, those who wished to make revolutions.

The former were the Utopians who drew up plans for allegedly perfect future societies but failed to work out the detailed mechanism necessary to realize their ideals within the historical process. The latter were socialists of the Blanqui type, who were socialists inasmuch as they believed in the victory of the proletariat and recognized that the real enemy was no longer the old aristocracy but the new bourgeoisie, but who looked to the

Babeuf–Buonarrotti tradition for their revolutionary methods:
that is to say, they separated the problem of the seizure of power
(by means of a conspiracy of initiates who were to set up a dictatorship in order to restructure the social order from top to bottom)
from the historical process which brings to fruition within
society the objective conditions necessary for revolution and the
will and participation of the masses. This meant that the followers
of Blanqui tended to place their emphasis exclusively on the
political aspects of the seizure of power, in contrast to Proudhon's
supporters who instead emphasized the purely economic aspect;
the Blanqui supporters tended to see the Revolution as a purely
subjective intervention in the historical process, almost as the
result of a global opposition acting from outside the existing
society, while on the opposite side were the many 'reformers' who
felt that socialism would be achieved within the society by a
series of corrective measures or by eliminating 'abuses' so as to
lift society on to a more perfect plane. Once again, both sides
grasped only one aspect of reality because socialism requires
overall opposition, not merely corrective measures, but it must
be an opposition arising from within the historical process, one
that is immanent in the contradictions of capitalist society.
Historicism and utopianism, political and economic factors,
overall opposition and internal transformation are all one-sided,
isolated, inadequate or false aspects of a complex reality that only
Marx was to express in a successful synthesis.

From the *Manifesto* onwards, he clearly shows that the
socialist revolutionary process takes place by virtue of an internal
mechanism intrinsic in capitalist society; it is the fruit of contradictions within that society and in particular of the basic contradiction between the forces of production, whose character
is becoming more and more marked, and the organization of the
conditions of production, which are in turn dominated by the
principle of private profit. Two years later, in 1850, he added a
new and important element to his theory of revolution, namely
that the contrast between the productive forces and the conditions of production can assume the violent form of a revolutionary
break only when the contrast becomes intensified as a result of
an increased imbalance within the capitalist society, that is, in
practice, as the result of an economic crisis; but he left somewhat
obscure the idea of a political crisis resulting from war, although
it was in his mind.

Marx's great historical value, therefore, was to have discerned
the revolutionary process within capitalist society as a dialectical

force inherent in the development of capitalism itself, inseparable from it and thus inevitable. Since it is also the result of the permanent contradictions of the system, the revolutionary process does not represent an isolated factor, an unexpected explosion; though it takes on more radical and more definitive forms in moments of particular stress in social conditions, of particular crises or imbalance. These radical forms, the breaks and rents in the social fabric, represent the culmination of a long process of continuous evolution, of ups and downs, effected not by a handful of conspirators or an enlightened *avant-garde* but by the main body of the proletarian army formed by those of the working classes who are more or less consciously involved in the struggle. The contradictions inside capitalism, the resulting class struggles, the ensuing transformation of social structures, the awareness of this historical process and its ultimate aims, the final exacerbation of the struggle and the collapse of capitalist society, these are the main features of the revolutionary process outlined by Marx, a process that is taking place as it were daily, which has moments when it seems to have stopped and periods when it is particularly acute, a process in which the daily struggle of the workers for the betterment of their living conditions overlaps with the revolutionary striving for a new social order. The link between the day-to-day struggle and the ultimate goal, between the objective factor of the contradictions in society and the subjective factor of the desire for revolution is a dialectical and not a mechanical one and the theories of the weaker brethren among the socialist leaders have almost always come to grief on this particular reef of the difficulty of grasping the dialectical nature of this link. It is here that their inability to direct the labour movement along Marxist lines, that is, to give it a serious and consciously revolutionary content, can be seen.

In the early days Marx's influence was exerted in at least three main ways: the assertion that the working-class movement must be autonomous and that there should be a clear distinction between the socialist and the bourgeois democratic parties; the insistence that this autonomous working-class movement should not remain isolated in the expectation of a revolutionary crisis but that, on the contrary, it should prepare for final victory when the crisis came by playing its part in the day-to-day struggle to extend democracy and satisfy its own class demands; and finally the conviction that the revolutionary crisis was an historical necessity bound up with the development of capitalist society itself. The first of these attitudes meant a clear demarcation of boundaries which led to a struggle on the right of the labour movement, *vis-à-vis* bourgeois democratic trends, and this was assisted by the class instincts of the masses; the second, however, implied a clean break both with the old ideas of Blanqui as well as with the anarchism of Bakunin, who was opposed to taking any part in the day-to-day political struggle and still dreamt of the final grand liquidation of bourgeois society to be achieved on D-day without any intermediaries, as a result of a decisive pitched battle between the opposing classes. The early congresses of the Second Internationale were dominated by these debates: it was almost a symbol of the dissension which was going to accompany the appearance of the socialist parties that the Second Internationale in Paris in 1889 – rather like the Italian Socialist Party three years later in Genoa – came into existence as a result of the clash of two simultaneous congresses, of which only the one which was mainly Marxist inspired proved capable of organizing itself to last. As for the boundaries which had to be drawn on the right, from the very first the congresses appeared quite clear at the organizational level, that is to say in the need to create an autonomous proletarian party (an area already occupied in Germany by the followers of Lassalle) but they showed themselves far less certain in the matters of ideological and political autonomy, which were supposed to be at the service of the organizational autonomy. In other words, what were to be the political aims and political action pursued by the socialist parties? While motions condemning any alliance or political collaboration with bourgeois parties were easily carried, great difficulty arose in finding criteria to distinguish future prospects, with the exception of the ultimate prospect of achieving socialism.

This gave rise to the central problem which is of the essence of any truly socialist movement: how does the ultimate goal affect day-to-day action and to what extent does it determine the line it should follow? There is an easy solution, at least in words, for any one who does not believe it worthwhile to participate in the life of the institutions of bourgeois society and sees the class struggle in terms of two opposing armies, face to face, scheming, awaiting the moment for the decisive battle: in such a case, the solution is to refuse to take part in any of the daily work of bourgeois society, a solution which is not only un-Marxist but unreal. For those, however, who believe in the usefulness and indeed in the necessity of such participation, the problem is more complex and can only be resolved in Marxist dialectical terms.

Where this dialectical skill is lacking and above all when, as a result of an appropriate emergency, pressure builds up in favour of direct action, both on the economic and political plane, there is a grave risk of a break between such action and the ultimate goal of socialism, that is to say that the present may jeopardize the future. When this happens, the boundaries drawn up by the labour movement on its right wing are obliterated; the organizational autonomy remains, as do the organizational boundaries, with the other bourgeois political groups, but the aims, methods, mentality and ideology of these political groups are taken over by the labour party itself, thus reviving motives within it that it had tried to exclude. Once this Marxist dialectical unity has been broken and the two factors of the day-to-day struggle and ultimate goals have once again become separate, there will continue to be a division between a possibilist, opportunist, reformist wing (whatever you like to call it) and a wing which is extremist, maximalist and intransigent; two facets of one of the same failure to understand the dialectics of reality, two political trends outside true class consciousness, and outside Marxist synthesis and revolutionary action in the true meaning of the word.

On the other hand it was inevitable that the practical side of the movement should react to the stimulus of possible direct action and would prove incapable of achieving that global vision of the historical process that was Marx's great contribution to political theory. From the time when, as a result of capitalist industrial development, the labour movement had begun to assume massive proportions, first in England and then gradually in the other countries of Western Europe, this urge towards direct action and practical considerations had become increasingly strong, but it was not aimed in just one direction because in reality the socialist parties had arisen as a result of the meeting of various social trends, each of them with its own needs and claims. In general we can recognize various trends in the history of the socialist parties, each having an historical continuity that pre-dates Marxism and which only the Marxist synthesis was capable of bringing together into a real unity. First of all there was, naturally, a proletarian trend that took on various forms: one was the radical revolt of the completely destitute against the whole existing social order; others, influenced more by economic or professional motives than by political ones restricted their action to supporting the demands of the trade unions and were not averse to an alliance with the party in power in order to

obtain their corporative advantage. In addition to these proletarian trends, there were also equally diverse ones of a democratic nature, formed mainly of petit bourgeois. Here you would
find democrats still more faithful to the tradition of 1848, and
finding it difficult to adapt themselves to the practical day-to-day
struggle. On the other hand there were the possibilists who
joined the labour movement because they saw it as based on the
masses and felt that it would provide the means of achieving the
final liberal-democratic compromise with the ruling class which
would ensure the political advancement of the lower classes of
society within the framework of the existing order. So, according
to the needs and aspirations of each of these various trends, each
tried to discover in the richness and complexity of Marx's doctrine
the specific aspect or factor that appealed to them most: some of
them looked for the autonomy of the working classes, others for
participation in the day-to-day struggles at trade union or political level, and yet others for the will to the ultimate revolution.

Only strong leadership and a constant endeavour to educate
based on the ability to draw the appropriate conclusions from
experience would have succeeded in realizing, in practical militant action, the dialectical synthesis that Marx had worked out in
theory, but had never been able to test by experience as a party
leader. Unfortunately, however, it was this capacity for dialectical
synthesis that was lacking in the leaders of the German Social
Democratic Party and the other parties claiming to be Marxist.
Of course, these leaders kept repeating that the day-to-day
struggle was only a preparation for the revolutionary crisis that
would arise from the process of capitalist development itself, but
this crisis was seen as something automatic, independent of the
action of the masses, as a natural rather than an historical necessity in the Marxist sense. But if it was a mechanical fact, a
natural necessity independent of the day-to-day action of the
masses, such action became purely narcissistic without any reference to the future revolution which it was not influencing in any
way and thus it remained an end in itself, enclosed within the
framework of capitalist society. After paying lip service to the
'future' revolution, the possibilists and opportunists could gently
lower their sights to the immediate target in view. On the other
hand, even the so-called intransigent revolutionaries failed to see
this link: for them the revolution was an inevitable catastrophe
bound up with an economic crisis which would inexorably occur
and for which they need merely wait without in the mean-
time dirtying their hands by pressing petty everyday demands,

and it was also bound up with the old 1848 formulas of barricades and uprisings, sudden seizure of power by force and the
physical occupation of their rightful seats. In the so-called radical
or revolutionary attitudes of the left wing of the socialist parties
there was almost no sign, even in the form of peaceful transition,[9]
of revolution conceived as a continuous process, as a constant
extension of power and a progressive shift in power relationships,
which was foremost in the thoughts of Marx and Engels, especially during the last decades of their activity.

Not even Karl Kautsky, the leading light of the theoretical
organ of the German Social Democratic Party, Die Neue Zeit, who
was regarded by everybody as the theoretical heir and official
interpreter of Marx's ideas, was a real Marxist: his Marxism was,
in fact, strongly imbued with the evolutionary positivism of his
period which had even succeeded in contaminating Engels himself
in his later years. Kautsky's later political evolution was, moreover, fully to confirm the fact that what Marx saw as a dialectical
synthesis between the day-to-day struggle and revolutionary
action was viewed by Kautsky as a mechanical contrast; the
actual struggle against opportunism and extremism, which in
Marx sprang from an original and independent view of the revolutionary process (and later on, in Lenin, from his remarkable feeling for concrete reality), in Kautsky took the form of flabby
centrism more like an attempt to achieve an eclectic reconciliation than a desire for clarification. The German Social Democratic
Party's Erfurt programme in 1891, largely Kautsky's work, mir-
rored this mentality, even if at first sight it might have seemed
true to the spirit of Marxism and was generally approved by
Engels himself: only by practical experience did it, in fact,
gradually become obvious that there was really no link between
the 'minimum programme' and the ultimate goal and that consequently Kautsky's eclecticism was a falsification of Marxist
dialectic.[10]

In practice the Social Democratic Party in Germany, and incidentally in other countries, became increasingly involved in the
struggle to achieve immediate objectives, the more readily since
the development of capitalism and its inner dynamism offered
new prospects of improvement in the living conditions of the
working classes and gradually eliminated the most serious causes
of discontent, thus creating the illusion of an uninterrupted
guaranteed economic and democratic advance. Satisfaction at the
success achieved in the realm of practical day-to-day affairs and
the hope of greater successes disguised the fact that socialist aims

were receding and these ultimate goals became increasingly
mythical, separated from the reality of the day-to-day struggle;
the dialectical synthesis of the two terms established by Marx
when he had shown the socialist revolution as growing out of the
development of capitalism seemed to have been completely lost.
One consequence of this situation, in which, as we have said, the
forces of objective reality and the failings and uncertainty of the
leaders came together was that the social democrats increasingly
turned into a bourgeois democratic party and lost sight of the
permanent link between the struggle to achieve democracy and
the struggle to achieve socialism, if indeed they ever properly
understood it. As a result they divorced democracy from socialism
and decided that each could be achieved in its own time and
place. It was distinguished from other middle-class parties by its
social composition, which was mainly working class, and its close
attention to workers' problems but it increasingly narrowed its
horizons and future aims to the limits of capitalist society and
thus to solutions compatible with the capitalist order of things,
thereby abandoning any desire to achieve the complete emancipation of the proletariat from capitalist exploitation. In a certain
sense, it was this working-class nature and close attention to
labour problems that helped to make the militants in the party
remain aloof from major political problems and fundamental
solutions. But as it did not succeed in breaking away from official
Marxist doctrine, there was a divorce between theory and practice, between its statements of principle and actual action which
led to an increasing predominance of revisionist ideas; and this
at least had the merit of providing the opportunity to theorize
which, though it meant a break with socialism, also meant a
reconciliation with the practical everyday experience of everyone.

The dialectical method

*From the point of view of methodology her writings
undoubtedly represent the best defence of Marxism
that anyone has produced.*

KARL RADEK

WHEN Rosa Luxemburg arrived in Germany in 1898 the debate
on revisionism, set off by Bernstein's writings, had just flared up.
She had hitherto been mainly involved in internal discussions
concerning socialism in Poland, principally at the national level,
and her contribution to this debate placed her amongst the
relatively small number of front-rank experts on Marxism. And
even today her reply to Bernstein is still a model of Marxist
methodology, markedly superior to Kautsky's, Plekhanov's,
Mehring's and others' criticism on this subject.[11]

If we accept Lukács' idea that Marxism's chief merit lies in its
dialectical method,[12] an idea with which Rosa Luxemburg is in
complete agreement, we can the more easily appreciate her contribution to the formulation of a modern Marxist strategy.[13] Rosa
Luxemburg's work, in fact, consists of an attempt to bring Marx's
dialectical method down to the level of the actual class struggle
and to make it not only a method of interpreting history and
analysing modern society but a method that can also be applied
to making history, that is to say applicable to the action of great
masses of people and the conscious shaping of the future. Unlike
many other Marxists, she experienced reality and history in
dialectical terms and, as she later wrote herself, she conceived the
dialectics of history as 'the rock on which the whole socialist
Marxist doctrine rests'[14] and as 'the specific way of thinking of
the class conscious proletariat', 'the intellectual weapon with
which the still materially down-trodden proletariat can overcome
the bourgeois by demonstrating their historically ephemeral
nature, showing that its own victory is inevitable and even now
achieving the revolution in the realm of the spirit!'[15] In other
words, it was thanks to dialectical methods of thinking that Rosa
Luxemburg was able to see a socialist future as already existing

in the capitalist present; this meant seizing on the contradictory aspects of present reality, which were indissolubly bound together, seeing the historical process that derived from their contradictory nature and realizing that the real essence of every movement can appear only if we consider that moment as existing within the continuity of history. But when we say history, we mean the total historical process; thus, just as various moments in time which are closely conjoined with each other in an endless succession cannot be artificially separated, so the various aspects of reality cannot be isolated either from the general context in which they occur and in which they mutually condition and influence each other.

This total conception is always Rosa Luxemburg's standpoint in considering any phenomenon and any event, and is, in fact, exactly the standpoint which Lukács, incidentally under Rosa Luxemburg's influence, considers to be the essence of Marxist method.[16] I am, of course, using the word 'total' in the sense in which Lukács, or to be more accurate, Marx and Rosa Luxemburg use it: it is a concrete totality, implying an organic nexus of relationships in which everything is related to the whole and the whole predominates over the parts. It is, of course, no fixed, static and immutable whole but one that is itself constantly being transformed. Hence any separation between politics, economics, law, morality and so on is an arbitrary one inasmuch as they are the various facets of one indivisible process (facets that can be distinguished as such but not abstractly divorced). Only someone conscious of this totality can understand the different factors which constitute this chain of events, can perceive their mutual relationships, their inner contradictions and their lines of development and only someone who can see beyond arbitrary divisions is able to study isolated phenomena and analyse them concretely.

This awareness of totality is always to be found in Rosa Luxemburg's analyses of social phenomena, and in her polemical works she had frequent opportunity to condemn her opponents' tendency to isolate phenomena and ignore the conception of totality. In her controversy with Bernstein which, as we pointed out, is largely a lesson on method, this criticism appears again and again: 'By abandoning scientific socialism he has lost the central intellectual axis around which isolated facts can crystallize as an organic whole in a global view of the world';[17] or: 'All the above-mentioned details of the theory of adaptation – apart from the fact that they all are false – have one further basic common characteristic. This theory fails to see all the phenomena of economic life which are being considered as organic elements in the overall development of capitalism but removes them from their context and sees them as having an independent existence, as *disjecta membra* [loose parts] of a lifeless machine.'[18] The same appeal to the sense of totality in the evaluation of phenomena recurs in almost all her controversies, whether with Lenin[19] or Kautsky. Kautsky, in order to justify the attitude of the Social Democrats during the World War, arbitrarily separated the period of war from the period of peace, as though the wars of the present historical era were not the result of the competing interests of the capitalist groups and of the need of capital to expand, and as though these causes were operative 'not only when the guns are thundering, but also in peacetime', thereby confirming Clausewitz's doctrine that 'war is the continuation of politics by other means'.[20] Thus she opposed all the Social Democrats when they supported the war as the right of self-defence against the threat of the Tsar.[21] Rosa Luxemburg, who was a leading member of two parties, the Polish and the German, and keenly interested in every aspect of the international labour movement, who indeed participated in it, held this profoundly international point of view based on the need 'for proletarian policy . . . to orientate itself internationally in the overall complex of the international political situation',[22] or again: 'the better we know these same social democratic principles in the full multiplicity of their different social milieux, the more we realize the essential principles underlying them and the further we can see beyond the horizon of any purely local viewpoint. It is not without reason that in revolutionary Marxism, internationalism rings out loud and clear and that opportunism is always matched by national particularism.'[23]

It could be said that the theoretical basis of Rosa Luxemburg's long struggle against revisionism and reformism is the constant reference to the concept of totality, which is the very essence of revolutionary Marxism, whereas the revisionists are vulgar empiricists who separate out isolated facts and fail to see the global nature of the historical process. For a Marxist grasping the totality of the historical process means seeing its inner contradictions and the need to overcome them through the victory of socialism; thus, in the practical struggle, it means never separating the isolated factors and isolated objectives of the struggle from the overall view of the struggle itself, nor the day-to-day activity of demands and reform from the future prospect of revolution, the 'ultimate goal'. This unity of the ultimate goal and day-to-day activity is the basic and central point of Rosa Luxemburg's strategy for the class struggle.

An idea of the great importance of Rosa Luxemburg's conception at that time can be seen by the fact that even today there is bitter disagreement within the labour movement as to the importance of the minor, day-to-day, battle and its relation to the final goal. For the nineties, Rosa Luxemburg provided quite simply the theoretical basis for a strategy for the struggle for socialism. It would, at a pinch, have been possible to construct such a theory from certain casual, barely perceptible remarks by Marx and Engels, but the whole of the trade union and parliamentary activity of Western social democracy in fact rested on mere empiricism, the dangers of which were very soon to be shown in the reformist movement. This fight against absolutism by a twenty-three-year-old girl in exile, in a position where Romantic ideas could all too easily gain the upper hand, was a marvellous achievement. It was an achievement based on serious study of revolutionary theories and of history, but at the same time it revealed a sure political instinct.[24]

Frölich's mention of Rosa Luxemburg's age refers to the report which she drew up for the international socialist congress at Zürich for the editor of the periodical *Sprawa Robotnicza*[25] emphasizing, in fact, the need for a conscious, controlled, global strategy; this need was reaffirmed even more clearly in a later report to the London Congress of 1896,[26] in which she drew particular attention to the chaotic nature of the Polish labour movement in the period from 1889–92 as a direct result of the failure to link immediate claims and long-term aims. However, it was not until her fight against revision and opportunism in Germany that she succeeded in elaborating and clarifying her revolutionary doctrine. At the first German Social Democratic Congress in Stuttgart in 1898, which she attended and at which she spoke, the question of the relationship between the day-to-day struggle and the ultimate goal was the central point of her argument.

The speeches of Heine and others have proved that within our party, one extremely important point is unclear, namely the understanding of the connection between our day-to-day struggle and our ultimate goal. It has been stated that the question of our ultimate goal makes an attractive item on our programme, and one that must not by any means be forgotten but it bears no direct relationship to our practical struggle. There may perhaps be a certain number of comrades who think that any speculation as to our ultimate aims would be an academic question. I claim, on the other hand, that for us, as a revolutionary and proletarian party, there can be no more practical question than that of our ultimate aims. Consider in fact what is the specifically socialist quality of our movement. The actual practical struggle falls into three parts: the trade union struggle, the struggle for social reform and the struggle for the democratization of the capitalist state. Are these three forms of struggle socialism in the true sense of the word? They are not . . . So what makes us a socialist party in our day-to-day struggle? Only the linking of these three forms of practical struggle to the ultimate goal. It is only the ultimate goal which gives spirit and content to our socialist struggle and makes it a class struggle.[27]

Speaking later at the same meeting, she concluded by inverting the famous saying of Bernstein's that the movement was everything and the goal nothing:

We must make reply to the latest speech by the Kaiser. We must say quite bluntly, like the elder Cato: 'On the whole, I think that this State must be destroyed.' Our ultimate goal is the seizure of political power and this goal is the soul of our struggle . . . The movement as such, without reference to the ultimate goal, the movement as an end in itself, means nothing for the working class, the ultimate goal is everything.[28]

Her two articles refuting Bernstein that we have already mentioned develop the same theme in depth: Bernstein's conception is mechanistic and not dialectical because it sees society and history not as forming an organically connected whole but as a mere series of facts, thus making it possible to abstract certain fixed causal relationships, to separate, like Proudhon, the 'good sides' of society from the 'bad sides',[29] to examine phenomena in isolation and to consider it possible to eliminate and correct other phenomena when they are in fact essential parts of the process of capitalist development. He thus feels that it is possible to divert the class struggle from its fundamental political aim of the struggle for power and to turn it into a series of unrelated actions so as to achieve isolated improvements in society that have no connection with the total conception of the struggle, that is to say, with the ultimate goal. And some twenty years later, when

explaining the Spartakus programme, she emphasized that the
contrast with the Erfurt programme lay precisely in the fact
that the former linked the ultimate goal with immediate
demands.[30]

> Seen from this viewpoint [wrote Lukács], by divorcing the
> movement from the ultimate goal, the revisionists are lapsing
> into the most primitive form of the labour movement. Because
> the ultimate goal is not something awaiting the proletariat at
> the end of the movement, independent of the movement and
> the path that it follows, a 'future State' situated in some vague
> place, a state of affairs which can thus be quietly forgotten in
> the day-to-day struggles and at most, produced in the Sunday
> sermon as a consoling factor in contrast to everyday cares.
> Nor is it a 'duty', an 'idea' which is introduced into the 'real'
> process as a regulating mechanism. The ultimate goal is, on
> the contrary, rather the 'relationship to the whole' (to the
> whole of society considered as a process), which alone can
> give every single moment of the struggle its revolutionary
> meaning. It is a relationship inherent in every moment, pre-
> cisely by reason of its simple everyday matter-of-factness, but
> which will only become real by becoming conscious of itself
> and thereby giving reality to each moment of the day-to-day
> struggle by revealing its relationship with the whole.[31]

If, however, Lukács continues, you try to keep the ultimate goal,
the 'essence' of the proletariat 'pure', you run the risk of losing
your concrete sense of reality and relapsing into extremism, a
childish but constantly recurring disease of the labour movement.

This last problem had not escaped the notice of Rosa Luxemburg, who had clearly recognized that the constant recurrence of
opportunism and extremism in the labour movement was caused
by the contradiction at the heart of capitalist society itself as
reflected in the labour movement.

> Marxist doctrine is not only capable of refuting oppor-
> tunism theoretically, but it is the only one capable of *explain-
> ing* opportunism as an historical phenomenon in the evolution
> of the party. The historical development of the proletariat
> before its final victory, is, in fact, not such a simple matter.
> The whole originality of this movement lies in the fact that for
> the first time in history the masses of the people are to realize
> their will through their own action against all the ruling
> classes but they must place this will beyond present society,

that is to say, go further than that society. But the masses can create this *will* only by continually struggling against the existing order and only within the framework of that order. The great problem of the social democratic movement is to give the great mass of the people a joint aim that transcends the existing order so that its whole development must steer a course between the two reefs of losing sight either of its mass nature or of its ultimate goal, between relapsing into a sect and falling into bourgeois reformism, between anarchism and opportunism.[32]

This passage of Rosa Luxemburg's is important not only to understand the dialectical nature of her thought but also to understand the root cause of the perpetual and ineradicable deviations within the labour movement towards reformism and extremism, opportunism and sectarianism; and she was certainly aware of the importance of her observation, since she repeated it almost word for word, several years later, in the course of her controversy with Lenin.[33] The meaning of the passage just quoted is that even the worker living in a contradictory society partakes of this contradictory nature and is simultaneously a member of the bourgeois society (and thus interested in providing himself with the best possible living conditions), and a member of the revolutionary class, the class which can only free itself from capitalist exploitation by destroying the capitalist order of things. And as the individual worker and considerable sections of the movement take into account *only* the day-to-day struggle for the betterment of their lot or *only* the ultimate goal, they will tend towards or indeed hurl themselves into one or other of the classical examples of deviation: in the first case they are neglecting the ultimate goal, that is to say, the need to direct every step of the movement towards the denial of capitalist society, and so are confined entirely within the scope of capitalism and are ultimately on bourgeois territory and in a subordinate position; in the second case they are spurning the day-to-day struggle and thinking only of preparing for the ultimate goal and thus becoming estranged from reality, frozen in dogma and sectarianism, separated from the vital flow of the movement until they fall into the extremist 'all or nothing' attitude, a dilemma which in reality has only one horn, which is 'nothing' because the 'all' can only be won by, in fact, preparing for it through the day-to-day struggle which they have rejected.

Some readers may be surprised that I attach such importance

to this statement of Rosa Luxemburg's which has been repeated so often as to appear completely banal; but anyone who is familiar with the history of the labour movement knows that it is this unresolved problem, this connection which has been so often sought after and never really grasped by the labour parties, that has given rise to so much strife, caused so many schisms and, above all, led to the progressive degeneration of German social democracy until its miserable demise on 4 August 1914 and, in turn, to the degeneration of all the Western socialist parties. The revisionists who want to revise Marxism by removing, as Bernstein suggested, 'the residue of Utopianism' from the ultimate goal under the pretext that this will restore its scientific unity and free it from the dichotomy of science versus Utopia fail to realize that 'Marx's dichotomy is merely between a socialist future and a capitalist present, between capital and labour, bourgeoisie and proletariat, that it is the scientific reflection on a grand scale of a dichotomy existing within bourgeois society, of the various bourgeois class antagonisms.'[34] In criticizing the day-to-day practice which pays lip service to the ultimate goal while tending arbitrarily to separate political and trade union activity and to acknowledge their mutual independence, Rosa Luxemburg pointed out that 'there are not two different sorts of class struggle for the working class, one of them economic and the other political but *one single* class struggle, which is aimed simultaneously at restricting capitalist exploitation within bourgeois society and abolishing it as well as bourgeois society itself'.[35]

However, she did not fail to realize that this abstract division between economic and political action, immediate demands and future socialist expectations, which in times of crisis is swept away by the intensity of the workers' forcible militant action, is bound to recur and intensify in quieter times, when the bureaucratic routine of the organization and of the practical daily activity of these same workers gains the upper hand over the creative capacity of the masses, above all with those workers who are already enjoying a better standard of living. As a result, Rosa Luxemburg regarded opportunism as inevitable in the labour movement. She saw it as one of two facets which are both contradictory and co-existent, the facet that is turned only towards the present moment, the facet that represents the immediate contact with bourgeois society which it is unable to grasp dialectically. This Marxist interpretation of opportunism gave Rosa Luxemburg a leading role in the great debate with Bernstein: in fact, it was not merely a question of correcting Bernstein's 'mistakes', as Kautsky was endeavouring to do, but of understanding the class basis which lies at the root of opportunism. Since the labour movement exists within bourgeois society and itself reflects that society's contradictions, it too represents contradictory aspects and one of them – empirical opportunism – involves the acceptance of the bourgeois mentality, in other words, it represents the presence within the labour movement of the class enemy, a presence to be resolutely attacked but the cause of whose recurrence cannot be ignored.

This is why Rosa Luxemburg was the most radical opponent of the opportunism and revisionism advocated by Bernstein, which she considered as non-socialist and 'when she was urged to consider them purely as conflicts within the socialist camp, she replied that on the contrary, it was a question of fighting the bourgeoisie whose influence was being introduced into socialism by revisionism';[36] nor did she delude herself that opportunism could be fought by organizational or disciplinary methods. As she wrote during her controversy with Lenin: 'it is a completely unhistorical illusion to think that social democratic tactics can be laid down in advance once and for all time and that the labour movement can be preserved for all time against opportunistic deviationism.'[37] The labour movement must be considered as a continuous process in which the two deviations of extremism and opportunism continually recur as a result of isolating the two terms of ultimate goal and immediate action, and it is by fighting these two deviations and thereby achieving dialectical awareness of the unity of its struggle that social democracy can succeed in working out a proper strategy. 'The proletarian movement did not become social democratic all at once, even in Germany, but it is *becoming so* every day, indeed, in the course of its continual endeavour to overcome the two deviationist extremes of anarchism and opportunism, both of which are merely factors in the social democratic movement conceived as a process.'[38] The German party had, in fact, moved from the need to fight extremist deviation, that is to say, from underestimating the importance of the day-to-day struggle and unduly emphasizing the ultimate goal as an end in itself to the need to fight opportunist deviation, which had led to overrating the day-to-day struggle and practically abandoning the ultimate goal.[39]

But what does 'unity of action' mean? What is the meaning of the statement that the ultimate goal, that is to say, the attainment of power in order to create a socialist society, is to be pursued even in the course of the day-to-day struggle? It means that the overriding criterion for every action of the labour movement, both in the realm of trade unionism and politics must always be a real step towards the goal, that at every moment the labour movement must have as its aims not the particular actions, particular measures and particular gains for their own sake but must always consider them in relation to the historical process in all its complexity. Thus any economic advantage, even a wage increase that might have to be paid for by accepting a political compromise strengthening its opponent's power as a class or furthering the plans of militaristic imperialism, must be rejected whereas a defeat at the practical level which nevertheless strengthens class consciousness may represent a step forward for the labour movement and ultimately turn out to be a victory.

If, on the other hand, we adopt the viewpoint of the bourgeois mentality which atomizes society, sees things instead of processes and tries to avoid the contradictions by isolating phenomena, if we are willing to consider that everything exists for itself apart from total reality, and ignore its links with the historical process, then any sort of bargaining is possible for the labour movement, but only at the price of abandoning the socialistic nature of the movement itself, which can only be a total vision. Such was the concept put forward by Heine, the deputy from Berlin, under the name of the 'theory of compensation', according to which the socialists ought to have voted in favour of the military estimates in Parliament in exchange for concessions in social policy and it was this concept that induced Schippel, another deputy, to advocate that workers and employers should adopt a common policy towards setting-up customs duties 'to assist the development of our industry'. Acceptance of these concessions pinpointed their ignorance of the fact that in exchange for immediate advantage on social policies or wage claims the socialists would not only have thrown away their parliamentary votes but helped to reinforce militarism and protectionism, that is to say two instruments of capitalist oppression and imperialistic development.

True

If we leave aside the insuperable contradictions and base ourselves purely on the fact that workers and bourgeoisie live on the same soil, we can come to an understanding on the so-called national interests, the protection of our national industry [v. Schippel's speeches in Hamburg], national 'defence' [v. Schippel again and his attitude towards the question of the militia], the Triple Alliance [v. Vollmar's speeches in Munich in 1891], a 'reasonable' colonial policy [v. Bernstein in his Bases of Socialism].[40]

Yet

In this way, opportunism while apparently introducing 'nothing new' into the party, in fact is, little by little, completely reversing the whole image of the labour movement. Its programme, tactics, attitude towards the State, towards the bourgeoisie, towards foreign policy and towards militarism, are turned upside down and from being a revolutionary international party, social democracy becomes a nationalist petit bourgeois social reform party.[41]

Naturally the opportunists, at least the overt ones, retorted by questioning the whole theoretical basis of Marxism itself

since our 'theory', that is to say, the principles of scientific socialism, fixes very firmly defined limits for practical activity, both as to the *objectives* to be pursued and the *methods* to be used in the struggle, as well as to the *type* of struggle. As a result, you will find amongst those who wish only to go chasing after practical success of various sorts a natural desire to have their hands free, that is to say, to separate our 'practice' from the theory, and make it independent.[43]

And unfortunately, as she was forced to acknowledge, the number of preachers of the 'gospel' of 'practical politics'[44] increased year by year and with every party congress. But as she added 'our movement has grown large and strong, not thanks to the "gospel" of so-called "practical politics" but despite it'.[45]

In this conflict between the vulgar opportunistic empiricism of the social democratic leaders and establishment and Rosa Luxemburg's Marxist vision of direct action, it was the former that prevailed, but historical events have tragically confirmed her prophecies: within a few years the slow but steady process of corruption had led the German Social Democrats to make common cause with imperialism in the 1914 War and after the war to prepare the way for Nazism as a result of their attitude. Yet at the time she was making her criticisms it was easy for her short-sighted contemporaries to refute her by accusing her of being doctrinaire, whereas vulgar empiricism could cloak itself in the garb of practical political realism, an attitude which Marx[46] had also denounced by comparing it to inshore coastal navigation, so often condemned by history yet impossible to uproot, since, as Rosa Luxemburg showed, its roots went deep into the very soil of bourgeois society and so could not be removed as long as this society exists.

The revolutionary class struggle against imperialism and the petit bourgeois opportunism that stems from it were the chief theme of Rosa Luxemburg's political activities. Yet a revolutionary class struggle can only be waged if every moment and every aspect of the struggle is related to the totality of the historical process seen in the light of Marxist methods.

> The essence of Marxism consists not of this or that opinion on current problems, but merely of two fundamental principles: the dialectical analysis of history, one of the central conclusions of which is the theory of the class struggle, and the analysis of the development of the capitalist economy. This last theory . . . is itself an exercise of genius in the application of dialectics and historical materialism to bourgeois economics. The heart of Marx's whole doctrine is to use the method of dialectical materialism to investigate the problems of social life, a method which recognizes that there are no constant or immutable phenomena, principles or dogmas . . . and thus every historical truth is submitted to constant and ruthless criticism, in the light of the real development of history.[47]

The obvious result of all this is that socialist action is conditioned by its knowledge of the historical process, of social development, in a word by a global vision. Only such a basis of close unity of knowledge and action, of theory and practice, can achieve success and only by continually asserting, in accordance with Marxist method, the indivisibility of reality and relating each single moment to this totality can the labour movement advance even in practical day-to-day matters in its economic and trade union struggles. And for her part, she always tried in her writings to develop an historical sense of the present, that is to say, the ability to analyse contemporary happenings, to discern the forces involved and the developments they were following, to separate the essential from the inessential, to unravel the most complex tangles, to evaluate mutual actions and reactions, thereby also discovering the hidden laws of the development of society and foreseeing some fundamental directions of the historical process.

Her historical analysis of the present was based above all on the recognition of the objective laws of development inherent in capitalist society. They are the laws studied by Marx which we do not need to examine here, if only for reasons of space. However, in her writings, Rosa Luxemburg hardly ever paused to reconsider, repeat or summarize Marx's doctrines, but endeavoured to apply them in a living context in her analysis of contemporary phenomena and the consequences that she drew from this for the purposes of action. In her writings, Marxism as she understood it was an unquestionable assumption and we would scrutinize them in vain to discover those long discussions on historical materialism, the primacy of the economic 'factor' or the political 'factor' or any other similar themes which were being widely discussed by the opponents and supporters of Marxism. In a short letter to Robert Seidl, who in a review of her doctoral theis on the industrial development of Poland[48] had taken up her point that Polish industrial development had been deliberately fostered by the government and had used this to assert the primacy of the political factor, she pointed out that even there the decisive element had been the economic circumstances, in the first place because it was economic considerations that had urged the government to promote industrial development and second, because it was only the general progress of the economy which had ensured the success of this policy of industrial development which, when it had been tried some decades before, had come to grief precisely because of the feudalistic form of national economy prevalent in Poland at the time. In conclusion, she added: 'If, therefore, there is undoubtedly a continuous mutual influence of economic and political factors in social change, the determining and decisive factor is, ultimately, the economic one.' Nevertheless, 'those Marxists who assert that economic development goes whistling ahead like some imaginary engine on the rails of history and that politics, ideology, etc. allow themselves to be left trailing passively behind like so many goods trucks would no longer be in line with Marxism'.[49]

Acceptance of Marxism is thus a necessary prerequisite for the socialist struggle.

> The greatest gain in the course of the proletarian class struggle was the discovery that the starting point for the achievement of socialism was to be found in the economic relationships within capitalist society. In this way, socialism, which for thousands of years had been dreamt of by mankind as an 'ideal', became an historical necessity.[50]

According to Marx, the revolt of the workers, their class struggle – and herein lies the guarantee of their strength and success – is merely the ideological reflection of the objective historical necessity of socialism.[51]

This deeply Marxist conception of socialism as an historical necessity led to Rosa Luxemburg's being accused of objectivism, determinatism and fatalism, as if she were confusing historical necessity with fate, an objective process independent of conscious human willpower. On the contrary, notwithstanding a certain crudeness of expression, owing partly to the fact that she was engaged in controversy and partly to the jargon in use in official German social democratic circles, her dialectical interpretation of history always excluded any idea of a mechanistic process, any predetermined interaction of cause and effect, and she never confused social laws with physical laws, whose effects can be calculated in advance; in a society where everything hangs together, in a process in which everything is linked and influenced by everything else and in which the human will is necessary in order to set the wheels of history in motion, the action of one law can be counteracted by another and a predictable effect can be cancelled out by new circumstances which produce the opposite effect. Above all, in such a contradictory society as capitalism, every phenomenon shows itself as two-faced and simultaneously sets opposing actions and reactions in motion, because it is society itself which encourages on the one hand the development of imperialism and on the other the development of the labour movement: 'world politics* and the labour movement . . . are merely two different aspects of the present phase of capitalism.'[52]

As a result, the laws of society are in reality *trends* which may thus very well not bear fruit.

Here, as everywhere else in history, theory can be of full use to us only by showing us the trend of a development, the logical conclusion towards which it is objectively proceeding. This final point can never be reached, any more than any preceding period of historical development has been able to follow completely through to it final consequences. And it is even less necessary for these consequences to be reached since social consciousness, this time embodied in the socialist proletariat, now plays an active part in the blind play of forces. And even in this case the correct interpretation of Marxist doctrine

* In English in the original.

provides this social consciousness with its most powerful stimulus and its most fruitful lines of development.[53]

'The correct interpretation of Marxist doctrine,' here is an invitation that should be pondered by all dogmatic Marxists who interpret all Marx's theses in a mechanical way. We may think, for example, of the mechanical and dogmatic interpretation of certain tendencies concerning the cost of labour which led a large wing of the labour movement to proclaim the dogma of complete impoverishment which is in no wise a Marxist conception.

> Only anarchists speculate on the increasing poverty of the masses as a result of which they must be logically considered as the political and theoretical representatives of the *Lumpen-proletariat*. Social democracy is always based on the rise of the working classes and the improvement of their conditions.[54]

Rosa Luxemburg on the other hand knows that trade union and day-to-day political activity are perfectly capable of achieving this improvement in absolute terms, even when this absolute improvement may mean not an increase but a reduction in the proportionate share of wage earners in the national income. Similarly, the conception of the State as a class State is valid as a trend.

> It has already become a commonplace to consider the State as at present constituted as a class State. But in our view even this concept, like everything in any way concerned with the capitalist State, should not be taken in any rigid absolute sense but in the fluid sense of an evolution.[55]

In this mutual interaction and conflict of trends which all correspond to an objective logical development, there is nothing either arbitrary or predetermined. Nothing is predetermined because there are no mechanical laws but instead merely trends that can be counteracted and because in the last analysis it is men's conscious effort of will that makes history and produces those very economic circumstances which then give birth to the objective trends. But nothing is arbitrary because man's conscious will is formed in the historical process, in action, in practice, in experience and in struggle, that is to say, that it is itself conditioned by the objective circumstances surrounding it and thus cannot be separated from the trends of development, from 'the logic of the objective historical process' that 'precedes the subjective logic of its protagonists'.[56] The 'logic of the objective, historical process', the 'logic of things' are expressions that frequently recur in her writings when she is asserting that history does not proceed in accordance with men's choice but contains forces within itself (created, of course, by men themselves), which nevertheless, once they have been set in motion, develop in accordance with their own dynamic laws. 'The English Revolution, after its outbreak in 1642' followed its course in accordance with 'the logic of things';[57] the Russian Revolution itself 'developed in accordance with its inner, fatal logic'.[58] 'The war, whose continuance Scheidemann and others are actively advocating, has a logic of its own, whose elected supporters are the capitalist agrarian elements which are in the saddle in Germany today and not those modest figures of the social democratic members of parliament and journalists who merely confine their activity to helping them into their saddle';[59] 'but things have a logic of their own even when men do not want to have any themselves.'[60]

So there is a logic of history, an objective historical process. But

the fact of taking the trend of the objective historical process into account neither blunts nor paralyses energetic revolutionary action, indeed it awakens and fortifies the will to action by indicating to us in which ways we may most surely direct the course of the development of society, warning us not to batter our heads vainly and hopelessly against the wall, an action which leads sooner or later to disillusionment and despair, and also preventing us from considering as revolutionary actions trends which the development of society has already changed into reactionary ones some time ago.[61]

So a revolutionary must recognize the objective trends of the historical process towards socialism in order to further them and spur them on without dispersing his own energy in a thousand ways that are, indeed, hopeless dead ends, already left behind by the course of history; but in addition he must recognize the opposing objective trends in order to confront them and block them. Thus war, though lying within the logical sphere of imperialism, can be prevented or halted by a conscious intervention on the part of the labour movement remaining true to its class policy, its policy of fighting against imperialism.

An effective guarantee of peace and a solid bulwark against war cannot be provided by pious desires, by cleverly compiled recipes or Utopian requests to the ruling classes, but only by the energetic will of the proletariat to remain true to its class policy and international solidarity through all the storms of imperialism. The socialist parties of the most influential countries and in particular the German Socialist Party were not lacking in requests and formulas but in the ability to support these requests and formulas by their will and action based on the class struggle and on internationalism;[62]

and it is as a result of their lack of courage or will consciously to intervene against the war-mongering policies of imperialism that German social democracy has become 'a rudderless hulk at the mercy of the winds of imperialism',[63] that is to say, dragged down by the logic of its opponents which they have been unable to withstand.

> Faced by the alternatives, of being for or against war, social democracy, the moment it abandoned 'against' was forced by the iron logic of history to throw its whole weight into the scale in favour of war.[64]

Yet it might have had the possibility and indeed the duty to make the opposite choice and rely on the objective forces that were working against war: this was Lenin's revolutionary policy in Russia.

But in Russia the socialist movement had already given proof of far greater energy and decisive determination and had shown the extent to which conscious human intervention can affect history.

> In Russia, it fell to the Social Democrats to replace a section of the historical process by their conscious intervention and to lead the proletariat directly from the political atomization which was the basis of the absolutist regime to the highest form of organization, as a class fighting for conscious aims.[65]

So nothing is more unfounded than the accusation of determinism or fatalism applied to a revolutionary like Rosa Luxemburg who emphasized the subjective factor in history so vigorously that she was forever quoting Faust's words 'in the beginning was the deed' and in the course of her bitter controversy with the so-called orthodox Marxists who went astray in their analyses of the Russian situation and failed to draw the appropriate revolutionary socialist consequences from them, she very properly recalled that

Marxism contains two essential elements: the analytical and critical element and the element of the active will of the working class as a factor of revolution. And any one employing only analysis and criticism is not representing Marxism but a pitiful, putrid parody of his doctrine.[66]

So it is not simply analysis without the will to draw the necessary conclusions for action but not even a revolutionary will unless based on an analysis of the situation, of the objective trends and forces involved: revolution becomes possible at a specific state of development, at a specific level of contradiction.[67]

The dialectical link between the objective and the subjective factor is moreover very clearly defined:

Men do not make their history of their own free will.[68] But they do make it themselves. The action of the proletariat is dependent on the state of development of the society of the time, but the development of society cannot be separated from the proletariat, it is both its cause and motive power as well as its product and effect. Its action is itself a determining factor of history. And if we are as incapable of skipping our historical development as a man of jumping over his own shadow, we can still speed it up or slow it down. Socialism is the first popular movement in the world which has as its aim and historical vocation to bring awareness, planned thinking and thus free will into men's social behaviour. This is why Friedrich Engels called the final victory of the socialist proletariat a leap by mankind from the animal kingdom into the realm of freedom. Even this 'leap' is linked with the iron laws of history, with the thousand and one steps in a painful and painfully slow evolution that has preceded it. But such a leap can never be achieved unless the living spark of the conscious will of the masses can be fired by the necessary objective conditions accumulated by evolution. The victory of socialism will not descend like fate from heaven. It will only be won by a long series of violent trials of strength between the old forces and the new, in the course of which the international proletariat, under the leadership of social democracy, will learn and strive to take its destinies into its own hands, to take over the helm of the life of society and far from being an impotent plaything of its own history, come to control it in full awareness of its aims.[69]

'The victory of socialism will not descend like fate from heaven': nothing could make it plainer that when Rosa Luxemburg speaks of socialism as an historical necessity, we must not understand this as meaning fatalism. And on the other hand, as we have already pointed out, by reason of the dialectical contradiction embodied in capitalist society itself, there exist today contradictory kinds of necessity. Historical dialectic in fact thrives on contradictions and for every necessity that exists in the world it produces its opposite.

> The dominance of the bourgeoisie is no doubt an historical necessity but so is the working-classes' revolt against it; capital is an historical necessity but so is its grave-digger, the socialist proletariat; world domination by imperialism is an historical necessity but so is its downfall by the proletarian Internationale. At every turn we meet two historical necessities that are in contradiction to each other.[70]

Which of them is going to prevail?

To her dying day, Rosa Luxemburg believed in the victory of socialism, yet she never tired of repeating that this victory would be no gift from heaven but only the result of a tough, conscious struggle by the masses. From the start of her activity as a publicist in Germany, she had repeatedly warned against the facile illusion of a speedy collapse of the bourgeoisie and pointed out that 'in addition to purely economic factors there are also political and historical factors affecting the rate of development of the bourgeoisie so considerably that they can blow skyhigh any carefully calculated theory as to the lifespan of capitalistic society'.[71]

And after twenty years of struggle, at the end of her life, she was more than ever convinced that the victory of socialism was not predetermined, even if it alone could save mankind from major catastrophes. The passage quoted above continues with these words:

> Our necessity will assume its rightful function from the moment when the other necessity of bourgeois class domination ceases to be the instrument of historical progress and becomes an obstacle and a danger to the further development of society. The present world war has revealed just this point in the capitalist order of society.[72]

Yet even in the months preceding her murder, in the blaze of revolution, she never ceased to issue the same warning:

The disasters into which capitalist society is plunging are not in themselves any guarantee of the victory of socialism. If the working classes cannot find the strength to free themselves, then society as a whole, including the working classes, may destroy itself by internecine strife.[73]

In her article on the Spartakus programme in the *Rote Fahne* of 14 December 1918, she wrote: 'Either capitalism will continue, with fresh wars and a rapid plunge into chaos and anarchy, or else capitalist exploitation will be abolished.'[74] And in her last speech at the founding congress of the German Communist Party, she repeated that 'if the proletariat fails in its duty as a class to bring about socialism, ruin will be staring us all in the face'.[75]

As can be seen, we are far removed from the scholastic interpretations of Marxism as a mechanical repetition of formulas and stereotypes valid at all times and places and in all circumstances. Precisely because nothing in history is predetermined, because the laws of evolution are in fact trends, because historical necessity strikes out in opposite directions and because the deciding factor, however much it may be objectively conditioned, is always ultimately deliberate human intervention, for all these reasons the data are always extremely complex, analyses need constant revision and trends of development have to be reassessed from time to time in order not to lose sight of that total concrete vision that Rosa Luxemburg considers the starting point for any revolutionary so that his own conscious intervention in the historical process can be made in the desired direction. 'Political events are not controlled by means of regulations but by becoming aware in advance of their foreseeable and calculable consequences and adapting your method of approach accordingly.'[76]

In application of this principle we find Rosa Luxemburg constantly attacking any interpretation of Marxism that seemed to her to be the mechanical repetition of formulas and patterns that failed to take into account the diversity of individual situations. Thus she criticized Lenin for his 'mechanical transposition of the principles of organization';[77] she reminded the Polish social patriots who always had Marx's well-known words on the independence of Poland on their lips that the only thing that really counted was the application of the method and basic principles of Marx's teaching and not 'turning a particular opinion of Marx on current problems into a dogma valid for all time, independent of the development of the historical conditions and not open to doubt or criticism';[78] in refuting the opponents of the general strike who based their arguments on an early work by Engels, she repeated 'the same approach and the same methods' may lead 'to different conclusions in different circumstances.'[79] After the 1905 Revolution when the Mensheviks were still trying to invoke the statements of Marx's Manifesto in order to prove the revolutionary function of the bourgeoisie and the need to support the bourgeois revolution, she pointed out to them that 'appealing to Marxs' and Engel's description of the role of the bourgeois some fifty-eight years ago and endeavouring to apply them to present circumstances is a gross example of the metaphysical approach which reduces the living and historical author of the Manifesto to rigid dogma whereas the dialectical thinking characteristic of historical materialism requires phenomena to be considered not statically but in movement'.[80] And referring to the 'apparent' competence and theoretical infallibility of 'official Marxism', that is to say, of Kautsky and company, she said that they were 'merely less distinguished theorists following on a master and clinging to his formulas whilst denying the living spirit of his doctrine'.[81]

The reader of Rosa Luxemburg's writings will find that these reproaches and accusations directed against dogmatic, mechanical, rigid and abstract interpretations of Marxism in general reflect her effort to apply Marxist methods to every fresh situation, to grasp the infinite richness of reality without losing herself in otiose detail but always going to the heart of things in order to give a vivid picture of the multiple connections that exist between various phenomena, in a word, to seize reality in its living rhythm, above all when it was a question of the rhythm of capitalist development or the growth of the labour movement: in this respect her exposition of the vicissitudes of the Russian Revolution of 1905 as well as various passages in her writings dealing with the war or her account of colonial conquest in *The Accumulation of Capital* all succeed in giving a remarkably clear picture both of the multiple facets of a phenomenon as well as of the internal logic that binds them together. Even her style, despite a certain old-fashioned verbiage, gives an impression of liveliness, of depth of feeling, of concreteness, far removed from the jejune, soulless and lifeless descriptions which so many of her and our contemporaries have inflicted on us under the pretext of Marxism.

And it is thanks to this method of hers that she succeeded not only in producing analyses confirmed by later events and in passing pertinent judgements on a situation but above all in prophesying future developments in the situation. She had no difficulty in foreseeing that the World War would result from the development of imperialism and thus, in the course of the First World War, she was able to foretell what would happen later, namely the victory of National Socialism and Fascism:

> More feverish rearmament by every State – with defeated Germany, of course, leading the field – and an era of unopposed domination by militarism and reaction throughout Europe, with a new world war as the ultimate aim.[83]

On this point too, history was to prove how right she was.

In a passage which I have already quoted, Rosa Luxemburg observed that the theoretical part of Marxist doctrine consisted of the dialectical materialistic analysis of history and the analysis of the development of the capitalist economy. I have already shown her view of the former so let us now rapidly examine how she conceived the latter.

The criterion she adopts for her analysis is the one that underlies her whole conception: it is the criterion of totality, as emerges clearly from her pamphlet against Bernstein. The latter had endeavoured to prove, with the aid of a lot of statistics, that Marx's prophecies had not, in fact, been realized: the bourgeoisie had not disappeared. The crises every ten years had not recurred, the concentration of capital had not taken place and so on and so forth. Some of these observations were unfounded, and later facts gave them the lie; others were based on a basic misunderstanding of Marxist thought. But what was interesting in Rosa Luxemburg's arguments was not the isolated details of her attack but the general trend of her reasoning. Capitalist society, she said, is an organic nexus of relationships with certain fixed and essential inherent aspects; among these essential aspects the fundamental one is the contradictory nature of this society, its inability to resolve its inner lack of balance. In his analysis, on the other hand, Bernstein had tried to draw the conclusion that capitalist society was gradually overcoming its own lack of balance which he considered as incidental (the 'disturbances' of the crises, the 'convulsive' reactions, etc.) and thus eliminating the process of self-destruction from within itself which was supposed to lead to the final catastrophe. Rosa Luxemburg's reply to this was that it does not really matter if crises do not recur at fixed ten-year intervals because the actual duration of the cycle is of secondary importance; what is essential is that capitalist society carries within itself an inexorable lack of balance between its capacity for expanding production and the possibilities of marketing its products profitably; it hardly matters if capitalist society succeeds in avoiding a self-destructive economic crisis, since the nature of the crisis that is to lead to the collapse of capitalist society is of secondary importance; the essential thing is that such a society, being unable to provide any definite remedy for its own contradictions, carries within itself the seeds of political and economic crises, that is to say of wars that can be turned into decisive crises by the action of the labour movement.

Since these contradictions are inherent in the nature of capitalism they will be aggravated by its development which will unfailingly accentuate the socialization of the productive process which is fundamentally opposed to the private organization of the conditions of production, and similarly accentuate its anti-democratic tendencies, so that even if certain secondary contradictions may change their nature, the fundamental character of capitalist society cannot be affected. Hence the classical petit bourgeois illusion that the good sides of capitalism can be preserved and the 'bad sides' corrected, an illusion found in Bernstein, is once again fated to reveal itself as such because the so-called 'bad sides' are in reality essential aspects of capitalist society.

> Fourier's idea of turning all the oceans of the world into lemonade by his system of phalansteries was extremely fanciful. But Bernstein's idea of turning the bitter sea of capitalism into a sweet sea of socialism by the addition of a few bottles of social reformist lemonade is no less fanciful, though more stupid.[85]

Once again it is apparent that reformism is not a path leading to socialism nor merely a longer process to achieve the same objectives which the revolutionary wishes to attain by seizing power. In fact reformism, precisely because it has lost its vision of capitalist society as a whole and is concerned merely with its details, has lost sight of the essential character of its contradictions and the part that they play in the whole complex of relationships in capitalism. For this reason it restricts itself to wanting to correct isolated aspects of society so as to mitigate its most striking contradictions, but by so doing it is adopting an attitude opposed to socialism which can only come about by exacerbating such contradictions, and above all by the proletariat's awareness that these contradictions are, in fact, insuperable. So even from this point of view it is the failure to relate to reality, that is to say to the sum of the relationships that make up capitalist society, that sharply distinguishes reformists from socialists and leads them to expend their efforts in the routine day-to-day struggle which uses up the workers' energy, dulls their revolutionary spirit and leaves them ill-prepared to cope with the major crises which may arise. If such crises are not turned into revolutionary events and used to destroy the bourgeois order of things (as the German proletariat failed to take advantage of the First World War), it is not because the Marxists were wrong in seeing the contradictions and crises of capitalist society and their destructive potential but because, with the help of the reformists, during the periods of quiet, the consciousness of the masses had been lulled to sleep; a break had occurred between the objective process of the development of society and the subjective process of creating such an awareness. Historically speaking, therefore, the reformists are the best allies of the bourgeoisie; as Rosa Luxemburg later wrote during the war, Krupp and German social democracy turned out to be the strongest supporters of German imperialism, because the former supplied the material weapons and the latter the spiritual ones with which to lull the masses to sleep and deceive them.[86]

Between her controversy with Bernstein and the outbreak of the First World War there was a period of some fifteen years during which Rosa Luxemburg had time to go more thoroughly into her analysis of capitalist society and show on the one hand its steady progress to the imperialistic phrase, its ever-increasing contradictions and the approaching tragic crisis of war, while on the other hand she showed that official social democracy was plunging more and more deeply into opportunism, restricting itself to immediate practical matters, losing any connection whatsoever with an overall view of social conditions and thus with its ultimate socialistic aim and, in the last analysis, seeing itself more and more in a subordinate role as a pillar of capitalist society.

I cannot here go into either her theory of crisis or the analysis of the process of accumulation of capital or, more broadly, into the general economic doctrines to which Rosa Luxemburg made such a noteworthy contribution (or one at least well worthy of discussion), since this book is concerned merely to point out her contribution to socialism's political doctrines. However, from this point of view, too, her analysis of the development of imperialism is of great importance.

Accumulation of capital, taken as a whole, as a concrete historical process, occurs in two distinct areas. The first is that of the actual production of the surplus value – in the factory, the mine and on the farm – and the sphere of marketing. Seen from this point of view, accumulation is a purely economic process, its most important phase being the relationship between capital and labour, whilst remaining in both its phases – manufacturing and marketing – exclusively within the limits of the exchange of goods – the exchange of equivalents. Peace, property and equality are the predominant forms here and it needed the sharp dialectics of scientific analysis to unmask the way in which, under the system of accumulation, the rights of property become the appropriation of other people's property, the exchange of goods becomes exploitation and equality turns into class supremacy.

The other area of the accumulation of capital is the world scene, where the protagonists are capitalist and non-capitalist forms of production. The predominant methods here are colonialism, the system of international loans, the policy of spheres of interest and war. Here violence, deceit, oppression, plunder and war stalk quite openly and it is not easy in this tangled web of power politics and overt violence to discern the iron laws of the economic process.

Liberal bourgeois theory sees only one side, the area of 'peaceful competition', technological miracles, the pure exchange of goods, and makes a clear division between this economic sphere of capitalism and its boisterous acts of violence which it regards as more or less incidental expressions of 'foreign policy'. In fact political violence is nothing but the vehicle of the economic process, the two aspects of the accumulation of capital are organically linked together by the need of capital to reproduce itself, and the historical cycle of capital can only be accomplished within this close relationship. Capital is not only born 'sweating blood and filth from every pore', but gradually imposes itself in this form upon the whole world, thus preparing its own downfall, amidst increasingly violent convulsions.[87]

This passage sums up almost all Rosa Luxemburg's essential views on the theme of imperialism. Above all, her basic methodical criterion is ever present: studying 'capitalist accumulation as a whole' and discerning 'in this tangled web of power politics and overt violence the iron laws of the economic process'. These laws exist and it is the task of Marxism – and its specific merit – to discover them:

Yet in this intricate web of competition and general anarchy, there obviously exist invisible yet fixed laws; otherwise capitalist society would have fallen into ruins a long time ago. The whole meaning of economics as a science and, in particular, the conscious aim of Marxist economic doctrine lie in determining these hidden laws that beneath the confusion of private enterprise economics, provide the order and unity of society as a whole.[88]

So it is the specific task of social democracy to carry on the same work of scientific systematization and discovery of the laws controlling the phase of imperialism as Marx had accomplished for the society of his time, a work which Marxists must never cease to perform in dealing with a concrete reality such as capitalism, which is never static; this theoretical work which is the task of one political party is, in fact, the other aspect which is inseparably linked with the practical revolutionary process, as Rosa Luxemburg never ceased pointing out.[89]

In her effort to grasp the ultimate laws of imperialist economics and pursue Marx's analyses into a new field, Rosa Luxemburg established her theory of accumulation as being a 'process of organic exchange between capitalist and non-capitalist methods of production',[90] this is to say that the surplus-value produced by capitalism cannot be entirely absorbed and thus transformed into a new source of accumulation and development of capital unless it utilizes non-capital formations, although at the same time it will destroy them as such. The absolute necessity of this process of exchange which, according to Rosa Luxemburg arises because it is impossible to use the surplus-value within the area of capitalism, is, of course, well known as being the most controversial point in Rosa Luxemburg's analysis of imperialism; nevertheless, leaving aside this question of absolute necessity, it is certain that Rosa Luxemburg showed rare powers of penetration in her analysis of the inseparable link between what she called in the passage quoted above 'the two areas of accumulation', that is to say between the process of capitalist development in highly industrialized countries and the attack on non-capitalist sectors, especially on peasant economies, and on colonialized or semi-colonialized territories.

It was particularly on this second aspect that Rosa Luxemburg concentrated her attention and though this sometimes led her to give a restrictive and incomplete definition of imperialism ('imperialism is the political expression of the process of the accumulation of capital in its competitive struggle for the residue of the non-capitalist systems which have not yet been taken over'[91]) it is certain that her analysis enabled her to penetrate more deeply than most into the real significance of international foreign policies of her time, the struggle for spheres of influence, for loans, the building of railways, etc., to unmask the mystique of Europe's claims as a civilizing power; to grasp, beneath the extremely complicated interplay of political, diplomatic and economic factors, imperialism's true nature as a greedy exploiter even in technically independent countries like Turkey, not to mention colonies in the real sense of the word; and finally to discover the roots of future world war in the internal dynamism of the capitalist society of her time.

Because, in fact, whether it is a matter of absolute necessity or not, this assault by the capitalist world on the non-capitalist world does correspond to an historical necessity of capitalism (a necessity which, as we saw, is always a trend rather than an inevitability), to its insatiable desire for expansion, accumulation and development, an assault of which it can at least confidently be said that 'an imperialistic policy is not the work of one or a number of States, it is produced when capital has reached a particular state of development and is by definition an international phenomenon, an indivisible whole that can be recognized only in all its inter-relationships'[92]; just as it can be confidently said that 'in its urge to acquire productive forces so as to exploit them, capital ranges over the whole world and obtains means of production in every part of the globe,[93] and seizes or acquires them at every level of civilization and in every form of society.'[94]

This imperialistic urge does not, however, work merely in the field of international politics; it is also active within the imperialistic countries themselves and strengthens and accentuates certain of their characteristics. One of these aspects of imperialism with which Rosa Luxemburg was particularly concerned throughout her whole life was militarism. Even in her anti-Bernstein article, she had emphasized its threefold function in the development of capitalism: first as a means of struggle by 'national' interests, competing with the interests of groups in other countries, secondly as the chief method of utilizing financial as well as industrial capital and finally as an internal instrument of class domination to oppose the working classes. As a result of this threefold function, militarism, even at the end of last century, already seemed to her destined to grow rapidly almost by a mechanical inner driving force of its own, until it reached the 'approaching explosion', that is to say, the greatly feared world war. 'As a result of the driving force of capitalist development, even militarism has become a capitalist disease.'[96]

Of the three functions of militarism mentioned above, two were being regularly denounced in the Social Democrats' political writings, namely that it was an instrument of international power politics and that it represented a bulwark of reaction and a force of repression aimed at the working class. It was Rosa Luxemburg's great merit that she particularly emphasized the economic aspect, that is to say that she showed that expenditure on armaments represented also an additional reliable market for capitalist production outside the normal functioning of the usual trade outlets.

> This constant supply of capital and living labour can be utilized for other productive purposes if a new and reliable demand can be found in society. This new demand is represented by the State with its share of the buying power of the working classes which it acquires through taxation. But the demand by the State is not for consumer goods . . . but for one specific category of product: instruments of war, for militaristic use both on land and sea.[79]

In addition a large number of modest demands for commodities, in small quantities and occurring at different times, which could be satisfied even by normal market production and thus would not help capital accumulation, are replaced by a State demand, forming one vast compact and powerful unity. But to satisfy such a demand you require a very highly developed heavy industry and thus the conditions most suitable to produce a surplus-value and accumulation of capital. So by means of State military contracts, the buying power of the masses of consumers, thus concentrated into one powerful massive block, is removed from the area of free choice and the subjective fluctuations of personal consumption and assumes an almost automatic regularity and a steady rate of development. On the other hand, thanks to the legislative apparatus of Parliament and the manipulation of so-called public opinion by the Press, the levers controlling this regular and automatic movement of war production are in the hands of capital itself. This particular area of capital accumulation would seem to enjoy unlimited possibilities of expansion. Whereas the extension of any other trade outlet or of the basis of capital operations largely depends on social, political and historical factors outside the control of capital, military production is an area where regular vigorous expansion seems rooted in and controlled by capital itself.[98]

Today, this function of rearmament to redress the permanent lack of balance between the rate of expansion of productive capacity and the rate of expansion of reliable demand has become a commonplace, and it is obvious that for the last quarter of a century America has preserved a relative equilibrium in its economy without running into dangerous crises thanks to its policy of rearmament. But at the time Rosa Luxemburg was making her analyses, these things were not obvious and indeed the Social Democrats themselves appeared more than reluctant to accept her argument which would have cast doubt on their whole political orientation.[99] As long as someone could in fact regard militarism as an instrument of international power politics, it was possible to hope that international conferences on compulsory arbitration and disarmament conventions might be effective just as it is possible to hope that poultices might be effective in curing abscesses on a body that is basically healthy. And naturally it was thought that on the day when international politics had reached the point of doing without militarism, internal politics too would be relieved of this imminent threat and the way would be clear for the complete victory of democracy. But if, as Rosa Luxemburg demonstrated, militarism still had an essential economic role and was an essential factor in the process of capital accumulation, any hope of limiting its monstrous growth was unrealistic and the prospect of peaceful democratic development was equally unrealistic because in order to fulfil its economic function, militarism needed the full collusion of heavy industry and poitical power, a collusion which in fact was to become increasingly an organic part of the structure of Germany under every regime, starting with the imperialist regime and continuing through Nazism up to the present day.

But if Rosa Luxemburg's analysis of imperialism destroyed the rosy Utopias of the social reformists, it opened up other hopeful horizons for the labour movement: not indeed the hope of a gentle collapse of capitalism but the much more realistic hope of a long hard struggle with the prospect of victory. On the one hand it was seen that militarism, the armaments race, colonial wars and the fierce struggle between the powers for control of markets formed an indispensable whole in the life and prosperity of capitalism in its imperialistic phase and that it was the height of

stupidity to shut one's eyes to these signs and rely merely on
the development of democracy or, worse still, to make a bargain
over armaments in exchange for a few modest social reforms. But
it could further be seen that imperialism represented an ever-
increasing burden for the working masses of the industrialized
countries as well as for the millions and millions of colonial
workers who were constantly being forced into the orbit of
capitalist exploitation. On the other hand imperialism, as it continually gave rise to new tensions and conflicts, offered the
historical opportunity for the political crises necessary to bring
the dissatisfaction of the masses to a head as a revolutionary
force. The more advanced this imperialistic process in fact is,

> the more the daily story of capital accumulation on a world
> scale will become a never-ending chain of catastrophe and
> political and social convulsions which, together with the
> periodical economic catastrophies arising from the crises, will
> make any continuation of capital accumulation an impos-
> sibility and the revolt of the international working classes
> against the domination of capital a necessity.[100]

From Rosa Luxemburg's analysis the two trends of development
inherent in this phase of society, the two opposing forms of
historical necessity which we mentioned above emerge clearly:
the trend towards world wars and catastrophes, that is to say
towards a clash between imperialist powers and the trend towards
socialist revolution, the decisive struggle between productive
forces and the relations of production, between the labour
movement led by the socialist party and the capitalist organization
of society. Imperialism is both an historical method of prolonging
the existence of capital and the surest means of objectively
hastening its end.[101] It depends largely on the attitude of the
labour movement, its ability deliberately to intervene, to turn
history in one direction or the other and bring about the triumph
of one or other of these historical necessities. So it was natural
that Rosa Luxemburg attacked most vigorously the Utopian ideas
of the social reformists, that is to say the illusion of being able to
'correct' the 'defects' of capitalism, to 'damp down' imperialism
through a policy of collaboration and the exchange of mutual
concessions between the proletariat and capitalism, the idea, in
fact, that the imperialistic phase is not an historical necessity, not
a decisive struggle for socialism but the wicked invention of a
handful of interested parties. This idea tends to persuade the
bourgeoisie that imperialism and militarism are harmful to them

from the point of view even of their own particular class interests, to isolate this alleged little group of 'interested parties' and form a proletarian block including a broad spectrum of the middle classes in order to 'damp down' imperialism, to starve it out by means of 'partial disarmaments', to 'remove its sting'! Just as liberalism in its decline turned away from the unenlightened monarchies to appeal to those that might be more enlightened, so the 'centre Marxists' would like to turn from the unenlightened middle classes and appeal to the middle classes that could be enlightened, from the catastrophic course of imperialism to international disarmament conventions, from the struggle of the great powers for world dictatorship by the sword to the peaceful federation of democratic national states. The general settlement of accounts to resolve the historical conflict between the proletariat and capital is turned into a Utopian historical compromise between proletariat and bourgeoisie in order to 'alleviate' the imperialistic conflicts between capitalist States.[102]

Unfortunately, it was this conception, which Rosa Luxemburg fought so passionately, that was going to prevail amongst the Social Democrats and determine their political attitudes. 'The unworthy successors who have been in charge of the theoretical development of the labour movement in Germany during the last decade showed themselves bankrupt as soon as the world crisis broke, and quietly capitulated to the imperialists': with these sad but unresigned words Rosa Luxemburg, writing from prison during the war, concluded her controversy with her critics on the subject of imperialism.[104]

Strategy

Marxism contains two essential elements: the critical analytical element and the active element of the will of the working classes. And anyone who adopts only the analytical approach does not represent Marxism but a miserable parody of that doctrine.

ROSA LUXEMBURG

WE HAVE been emphasizing the importance of Rosa Luxemburg's dialectical method and the significance of her continual reference to totality because these are the keys not only for the understanding of her constant attacks on revisionism but of her revolutionary strategy based, as we saw, on re-establishing dialectical unity between day-to-day action and the ultimate revolutionary goal.

In this respect social democratic thought was undergoing a profound crisis in the final decade of last century when the practical approach was beginning to expand so successfully. It was the Bernstein controversy which forced the German Social Democrats to come to terms with (but not to solve) a whole series of problems which existed quite apart from Bernstein and which can be summed up as the discrepancy between social democracy's official theoretical utterances and its real practical activity. In theory, the Social Democrats acknowledged themselves as followers of Marxist doctrine, above all through the influence of Engels, who was watching the movement closely from London, and of Kautsky who had been editor of the periodical *Neue Zeit* since 1883 and was using it in his struggle to achieve the victory of Marxism. Among the party leaders, Wilhelm Liebknecht was a Marxist and August Bebel, chairman of the party up to the outbreak of the First World War, although he had taken Lassalle as his starting point, later went over to Marxism. However, through the fault of Engels in his later years but above all because of Kautsky, the Marxism which had been assimilated by German social democracy had lost a great deal of its dialectical edge and revolutionary force and as one's temperament or circumstances dictated, it was interpreted as a revolutionary messianic belief or as theory to justify participation in elections or in the petty day-to-day struggle. The Erfurt programme of 1891 tried to reconcile these twin needs by adopting a theoretical approach based on revolutionary formulas and a programme of minimum action but without really combining the two. The minimum programme was also less suitable for preparing the way for a revolutionary crisis than for waiting for such a crisis, whereas the theoretical programme was unable to lay down a proletarian strategy and left the question of the seizure of power unclear.[105]

The result of this inability to balance the two factors was that the revolutionary aspect became more and more anemic and divorced from reality whilst the party concentrated more and more on the practical day-to-day struggle. Even around 1890 the prospect of revolution seemed very close to the social democratic leaders and could even be calculated 'with mathematical certainty';[106] and, at the Erfurt meeting, Bebel said: 'I am convinced that the realization of our aims is so close that there are few people in this hall who will not live to see it.'[107] But since at the same time the Social Democrats had abandoned the idea of fighting in the streets, the prospect of revolution was dependent either on a collapse of the capitalist system, that is to say by an independent cause based on a severe economic crisis, or else on their success in achieving a parliamentary majority.

But the first alternative seemed just then to dissolve into thin air; Germany was in a period of economic prosperity. From ranking fourth among the industrial countries of the world, she had risen to third by about 1890 and to second by around 1900. Industrially the country was changing very fast: in the iron, steel and coal industries, the process of concentration reigned supreme as well as in the chemical and electro-technical industries. The foundation for an imperialist policy was thus laid, a policy which was to find expression in foreign trade, the acquisition of colonies, world affairs and in the armaments race. The other side of this capitalist expansion was the increase in real wages which, although still low, gave the lie to the current theories of progressive impoverishment, and the development of social security which had already been planned by Bismarck and showed the masses the paternalistic side of the State. The possibility of a disastrous economic crisis and even of any sort of a crisis seemed ever more remote, even to the socialists; the Marxist theory of crisis seemed to have suffered a grave blow.

In many people's eyes only one road to power seemed possible:

achieving a political majority in Parliament. As early as 1893 Mehring was protesting against such a Utopian view in the *Neue Zeit*:

> The view that a majority in a bourgeois Parliament, even if it consisted of class conscious workers, can prepare the way for a socialist society, is a knife which has neither blade nor handle. Only once belief in bourgeois Parliamentarism is completely dead amongst the masses can the way to the future open up.[108]

But Kautsky had denied this[109] and even Engels had frequently confessed his enthusiasm for the Parliamentary system. But experience was to show the core of truth in Mehring's attitude, if you look upon it as, in fact, not a refusal to accept Parliamentary struggle but as a denial of its ability to lead to socialism. The acceptance of the Parliamentary system by the socialist parties no doubt contributed to a considerable extent to the victory of opportunism: in order to win seats in Parliament, the party had to extend its influence over far wider sections of the population and as often happens this did not mean persuading these sections of the justice of the socialist cause but adapting socialism to the mentality and practical needs of such sections of society. But if the parliamentarization of the party drove socialist objectives further into the future rather than bringing them closer, it did allow more immediate aims to be pursued as a result of the increasing influence of the party.

Finally, this hope of achieving a Parliamentary majority established a link between the day-to-day struggle and the ultimate goal, while yet allowing the party to concentrate exclusively on the present, since the future was merely the sum of the many minor successes which were being recorded in every electoral region of the German Reich. During this period, the two basic components of revisionism can be plainly seen: on the one hand, the possibility of exploiting economic crises to improve the standard of living, thereby arousing increased interest in those directly and practically concerned in the day-to-day struggle; on the other, the hope of using the representative bodies in order to increase the influence of the party on the political power. Inasmuch as these two motives combined to an increasing extent to satisfy immediate real needs and produce progressively more bearable living conditions for large sections of the masses, the prospect of revolution became less interesting and the workers directed their efforts increasingly towards immediate ends, ends that lie within the orbit of capitalist society: the Social Democrats' subordination to capitalism appeared obvious even at that time, despite the repeated confessions of faith made at every party congress.

When Bernstein began writing his articles, the party's actual practice was already dominated by opportunism. Since 1891 von Vollmar, the Chairman of the Bavarian Social Democrats had made two speeches in favour of a possibilistic approach emphasizing, in fact, the immediate tasks.[110] 'Social democracy', he said, 'must abandon "theoretical" discussions about tomorrow in order to concentrate its whole effort on the most immediate and urgent concerns'; at the same time he paid the price for his possibilism in accepting the government's foreign policy, acknowledging the Triple Alliance as a contribution to peace and allowing it to be understood that in case of war social democracy would contribute to the defence of the country. We can already see the germ of the Social Democrats' steady retreat from principles that culminated in their surrender in 1919. Yet when von Vollmar was attacked for the theses that he was supporting, he retorted with some justification that he was merely describing what was already being practised by the party and this judgement was to be confirmed by the most recent historians:

> Revisionism is merely a weak reflection of these very general reformist practices. It was not Schippel, Bernstein, Heine, Calwer or Hildebrand but von Vollmar, Grillenberger, Auer, Kloss, von Elm, Legien, Leipart, Hué, Dr Südekum, Ebert, Scheidemann, Keil and Löe, not the revisionist academics of the *Sozialistische Monashefte* but the labour secretaries and trade union leaders, the local politicians and the Landstag representatives, all those who were ultimately impregnable because they were irreplaceable, since they were responsible for everyday routine, who determined the character of the party which by 1900 had declined into being an essentially practical labour party with a few revolutionary phrases tacked on which were not taken seriously.[111]

This trend was especially reinforced by the south German provinces where industry and thus the working classes were less advanced and votes had to be found amongst the petit bourgeoisie and peasants; for this reason, von Vollmar, who was a Bavarian, had adopted an agrarian programme adapted to the interests of the large and medium farmers. Thanks to this policy of adaptation, the party succeeded in winning votes and its class basis was less apparent as new sections of the petit bourgeoisie rushed to

join, partly to further their careers and ambitions and partly because they were attracted by the bourgeois democratic function
which the party had come to represent. And by 1892, barely two
years after the repeal of the emergency regulation, Hans Müller
was able to speak of a class struggle within the Social Democratic
Party. He noted that certain elements had entered the party who
lacked any revolutionary feeling or proletarian sympathies, sections of society who have no idea of radically abolishing the
existing economic order but of procuring better positions within
it'.[112] So while the party leaders continued to use the traditional
terminology and paid the obligatory lipservice to Marxism, during
these years the party underwent a profound transformation,
above all under the pressure of the representatives of the local
bodies, the provincial officials and the trade unionists. While the
parliamentary group in the Bavarian Landstag was already voting
for the budget as early as 1894 and was censured for so doing at
the next national congress of the party, the Social Democrats in
Baden started extensive experiments in collaboration, at a local
level, with the ruling middle-class parties. At the same time the
trade unions tried to get rid of the theoretical and political control
by the party; at the Trade Union Congress in Frankfurt, Theodor
Leipart was echoing a widely held opinion when he said, 'Let us
quietly advance into bourgeois society and as citizens with equal
rights defend our own rights and claims like all other classes
and parties.'[113] Logically enough, the more the socialist hope of
realizing long term aims was abandoned, the stronger the trend
towards improving present living conditions was to become;
the break between future and present became more and more
definite.[114] And naturally enough the average party official only
occupied himself with the present which immediately concerned
him.[115]

The process took place more slowly but equally plainly in the
Reichstag where the party had to take account of its traditions,
the vigilance of its more knowledgeable members and the decisions reached at its congresses. None the less, here too the
revisionist offensive against the official party line took place; it
could be said that in every electoral contest the desire to broaden
the basis of the electorate brought not only more breaches in the
party doctrine but also in party policy. Max Schippel was the
initiator in this when he approved the need to accept the military
estimates to reduce the dangers facing German soldiers in case
of war; in support of this thesis the Berlin deputy, Heine, evolved
the theory of 'compensation' whereby the Social Democrats

should buy concessions in the field of social policy in exchange for their agreement; then Schippel made a speech supporting a common policy of workers and employers to establish protective customs duties. Although the party in general condemned these attitudes, their revisionist spirit eventually permeated of its own accord the whole day-to-day policy of the party and thus produced the official split between theory and practice that Bernstein was in fact trying to bridge when he tried to revise Marx's doctrine.

By doing this he, in fact, provoked an open conflict. Even though the leaders could hitherto pretend that they were unaware of the revisionist nature of their conduct of affairs and plaster over with the usual phrases the split between theory and practice, day-to-day struggle and ultimate goal, present and future – a breach which the Erfurt programme had failed to overcome – Bernstein's excursion into the theoretical field forced them to take an open stand. One of the older leaders, Ignaz Auer, who was unequivocally on the right wing of the central committee of the party, had indeed clearly seen this when he wrote to Bernstein:

> Do you really think it possible that a party whose writings go back fifty years, whose organization goes back almost forty years and whose tradition goes back even further can change its direction like this at the drop of a hat? My dear Ede, what you're asking is not something that you *decide on*, not something that you *say*, but something that you *do*. Our whole activity – even when that shameful regulation was operating – was that of a social democratic reform party. A party that takes account of the masses can in fact never be anything else.[116]

In the event, even Bernstein went to work cautiously. Between October 1896 and 1898 he published a series of articles in the *Neue Zeit* under the title 'Problems of Socialism' in which his criticism of Marxism was at first implicit, not explicit. In January 1897 the attack was directed against the party's intransigent tactics and in favour of a tactic of compromise; but then Bernstein moved on to a criticism of the concept of class, of the crisis theory and so on. Finally in January, 1898, in an article entitled 'The Theory of Collapse and Colonial Policy' replying to Belfort Bax, who had asserted that Bernstein had abandoned socialism's ultimate goal, he came out plainly with the statement that he was not at all interested in what was commonly called the ultimate goal and wrote the sentence that has become famous: 'The ulti-mate goal, whatever it may be, means nothing to me, the move-ment means everything.'

The dull routine inherent in this proposition could find no favour with Rosa Luxemburg. She came from Poland, a country only slightly industrialized and which in addition formed part of the Russian Empire, that is to say an Empire that had abolished serfdom only a few decades earlier and was taking its first steps towards industrialization, while still under the domination of precapitalist political absolutism. As a young girl she had partici-pated in illegal movements in her own country and so she brought with her to the west the revolutionary impetus of the milieu in which she had grown up; on the other hand, her Jewish cosmopo-litanism, her liveliness of mind, her economic studies at the University of Zürich and finally her practical militant experience in Germany made it possible for her to overcome the limitations of her original milieu and adapt to western conditions without losing the revolutionary spirit which had burned in her from her earliest youth.

Since she continued to play an active and responsible role in two parties, the German and the Polish, that were operating in such different conditions, as well as following the labour move-ments in every other country because of her deep sense of inter-nationalism, she could not have been better placed in the attempt to produce a synthesis of these varied experiences and especially of the two basic ones, that of a developed capitalist society where the primary consideration, despite all the revolutionary speeches, was day-to-day action and the opposite experience of a country whose objective situation left little room for day-to-day action and encouraged violent revolutionary change and the old forms of conspiratorial activity. Because its roots were in the Russo–Polish movement, Rosa Luxemburg's radicalism was quite different in character from that of the German radicals, with the one exception of Liebknecht. Revolution was never absent from Rosa Luxemburg's mind, and preparing the revolution was, in Clara Zetkin's words, 'her only ambition'. She tried to inculate Western European social democracy, and above all, the German party, with this ambition. At the same time, as her controversy with Lenin showed, she tried to make the essence of democracy comprehensible to the conspiratorial Russo–Polish movement, and by the 'essence' of democracy, she meant the dignity of every man and his ability to collaborate in the shaping of his own fate.[118]

This revolutionary tension together with her unbending nature made it particularly difficult for her to become acclimatized to the atmosphere of German social democracy, where there was certainly no breath of revolution and this made the task of her internal opponents easier. Amongst the 'fathers of the party' in the SPD, Rosa Luxemburg was liable to alienate rather than arouse a feeling of trust and good will, as she was temperamentally so foreign to German ideas and her uncompromising ideals tore the veil of routine from people's eyes and broadened and enlightened their horizons. After a while, however, even they were forced to admit that Rosa Luxemburg was no mere bright brief meteorite but a person genuinely and totally bound up in the labour movement with every fibre of her being. This impression prevailed even if there always remained a slight feeling of strangeness when faced by this militant politician who never made any concessions to routine but always sought for a solution, the way out of any given situation. Just as she was the first to realize that the canker had already begun to penetrate within the ranks of that great and powerful party which was, at that time, the hope of the whole labour movement, and that it was already being attacked by the worm of opportunism, she was also the first to shake the leaders of the party out of their complacency.[119] And in fact she was not only the first expressly to denounce Bernstein's overt revisionism as being a manifestation of a bourgeois way of thinking and as revealing the class enemy among the ranks of the proletariat, she was also the first to lay bare the revisionism and opportunism hidden under the mask of Marxist orthodoxy, that of the leaders as well as that of the pseudo left-wing radicals themselves who never did anything but pay constant lipservice to the sanctity of principles.[120] If for tactical reasons she was often obliged to use in her controversies the words used by the leaders themselves and thus pretend to approve them, her letters provide clear proof of her real thoughts.

From the time of her first contacts with the German Social Democrats we find her writing to Robert Seidl in Zürich[121] denouncing the 'conventional, wooden and stereotyped' nature of the articles being written there, and a few years later she wrote quite openly to the same correspondent about the official world of the party which did not even allow the truth to appear in the socialist newspapers. The following year in a letter to her friend Roland-Holst, she gave vent to her ill-humour against the political attitude of this official world, apparently radical but increasingly stereotyped and soulless.

I am not at all enthusiastic [she wrote] about the role played hitherto by the so called orthodox 'radicalism'. Tracking down isolated opportunistic stupidities and incessantly criticizing them is not the sort of work I enjoy, in fact I am so thoroughly fed up with it that in such cases I much prefer to keep quiet. I also admire the self-assurance with which a number of our radical friends always find it necessary to bring the lost sheep – the party – back into the safe fold of 'sound principles' and fail to appreciate that we're not advancing one single step by behaving in this negative way. And if a revolutionary movement is not going forwards, then it's going backwards. The only way to fight opportunism root and branch is to go forward oneself and develop tactics to increase the revolutionary nature of the movement. Opportunism is in fact a bog plant that grows fast and thrives in the stagnant water of the movement and wilts in a strong, lively current. Here in Germany there is a really urgent and burning need to go forward. And there are very few people who feel it. Some of them continually disperse their energies in petty skirmishes against the opportunists, others believe that an automatic and mechanical increase in numbers (in the elections and in the organization) is the same thing as going ahead. They forget that quantity must be replaced by quality and that a party which is three million strong can no longer make the same automatic gestures that a party of half a million used to make. I don't need to tell you that of course I'm not thinking of suddenly 'coming out on to the street' or of any other sort of artificial venture. But the whole of labour must strike a deeper note, it must become increasingly aware of its own strength and . . . but I'll stop there before my letter becomes a leading article.[122]

A little later on, as the result of the Russian Revolution and the debate on the general strike, she began to turn away from Kautsky when she realized his limitations and the contradiction between his words and his deeds; in a letter written to Clara Zetkin in 1907 she also expressed herself bluntly on Bebel, the undisputed leader of the party, and on the party which he led.

Since my return from Russia I feel rather isolated . . . I'm bitterly and painfully conscious of the pusillanimity and pettiness of the whole party more than ever before. But I don't get so excited about this as you do because I've already realized with terrifying clarity that these things and these men cannot change until the whole situation has changed and even then . . .

we must quite simply expect that these people are bound to oppose us if we are to carry the masses forward with us. The situation is quite simply this: August [Bebel] and the others even more so have handed themselves over lock, stock and barrel to Parliamentary government. At any turn of events that goes beyond Parliamentary government, they are completely at a loss, indeed, even worse, they endeavour to bring everything back into the confines of Parliament and so ferociously attack everyone and anyone who wants to work outside Parliament as 'enemies of the people'. I feel that the masses and even more the great mass of comrades are inwardly fed up with Parliamentary government. They would greet the introduction of a breath of fresh air into our tactics with enthusiasm but they still have the old pundits weighing them down and the leading opportunist journalists, deputies and trade unionists even more so . . .! As long as it was a question of defending them against Bernstein and Co, August and Co quite liked our company and our support because left to themselves they made a proper mess of it. But when it comes to launching an offensive against opportunism then all the old hands join forces with Ede [Bernstein], Vollmar and David against us.[123]

These judgements by Rosa Luxemburg have more political than personal importance because they show that behind Kautsky's and Bebel's Marxist formulas and class-conscious pronouncements there already lurked a hidden acceptance of reformist action. Moreover, as we shall see, Rosa Luxemburg's revolutionary and reformist attitude lay not so much in the 'what', that is to say in the objectives of the day-to-day struggle as in the 'how', that is to say in the linking of these objectives to the ultimate goal. When this link is lacking, despite all verbal protestations, if the ultimate prospect of socialism has no influence on the so called 'minimum programme' and the latter is merely an end in itself, then in fact the official party line became confused with the revisionist line. Against this, Rosa Luxemburg's revolutionary line – despite the legend spread by her opponents of 'bloodthirsty Rosa', of 'a revolutionary Romantic' (Piero Gobetti, completely misjudging her, even called her outright a 'Romantic incendiary') – was a Marxist line based on careful study and political realism. During the World War, when she had completely broken with the official Social Democratic Party and felt the post-war revolution approaching, she still praised the new Marxist strategy that had replaced barricades by study but on condition that 'the hour-to-hour tactical struggle must be directed to the immutable final goal'.[124] Her attack on the Social Democrats' practice was in fact based on their failure to direct their day-to-day struggle towards the ultimate goal.

We must now try to make clear the basic difference between the two conceptions; and first of all, it is important to recapitulate what has already been said about the difference between an evolutionary and a dialectical view of history. The first of these, which largely dominated social democratic thinking, regarded history as developing in a straight line with socialism succeeding capitalism as inevitably as one station follows another on a railway line. Even for those who had not abandoned the socialist ideal and sincerely believed that they were working for it, this work consisted merely of making occasional small steps forward, either in the form of economic or political gains, each step representing a definite approach to the goal. And in this conception, the goal was not a revolutionary upheaval but the gradual, progressive and almost imperceptible transformation of present society into a socialist one. For this reason, every effort had to be made to reduce the conflicts, blunt the issues, find compromises, not exacerbate situations and avoid acute emergencies so that history should continue to advance and, provided you were patient enough, you would move on from the capitalist to the socialist station. At the most you must find a way to prevent your opponents from pushing the course of history backwards: in this sense, it can be said, as Schorske put it, that Bebel's tactics were defensive and even the references to violence and to a general strike that occur in his speeches form part of a defensive attitude.[125]

Rosa Luxemburg's conception was the exact opposite: for her, history is not linear but proceeds by dialectical contradictions, via the class struggle. As we have seen, historical necessity does exist in the sense that history cannot be made arbitrarily, it is not a business where you can buy what you want[126] but where the present always conditions the future. Nevertheless, since this present is always contradictory the present society is torn by class conflict, it contains contradictory trends; imperialism and socialism are both objective tendencies of the development of society. For that reason, if you want the socialist trend of historical development to prevail over the other, you must fight hard at every stage but you must do it in a rigorously scientific way, that is to say you must first analyse the objective trends of the development of society,[127] isolate their revolutionary elements[128] and press forward strongly in that direction in such a way as to increase both the conflict with the ruling class (which is of necessity pulling the development of society in the opposite direction) as well as the revolutionary consciousness of the masses.[129] So it is not a matter merely of possessing one's soul in patience but of acting.[130] Obviously even for Rosa Luxemburg there are moments of greater or less tension, the struggle has its ups and downs, but there can never be any halt in the absolute meaning of the word because the situation always offers opportunities and incentives for agitation and strife. It is even more inadmissible to want to avoid open struggle in moments of crisis: 'It is mad folly to imagine that we must merely survive war, like a rabbit under a bush waiting for the storm to come to an end and then happily setting off on its way again,'[131] she wrote in an attack on Kautsky's 'wait and see' attitude. And since history does not develop in a linear but in a contradictory, uneven and thus diverse way, situations never repeat themselves identically and it is impossible to try to apply remedies and formulas that are valid for every case, as the bureaucrats in the organization and the narrow-minded supporters of 'nothing but Parliament' want to do; the struggle must always be a concrete one based on an unprejudiced analysis capable of grasping the living, changing reality of class relationships and power situations.

The modern proletarian class does not wage its struggle in accordance with a ready-made plan contained in a book or in a theory. The modern workers' struggle is a piece of history, a piece of historical development. And we are learning how to fight in the midst of history, in the course of the development, in the midst of the struggle . . . The first duty of militant politicians like ourselves is to go forward together with the development of the times and to be conscious every minute of the changes in the modern world and in our battle strategy.[132]

Thus, no preconceived plan, no fixed pattern but also no empiricism. On the contrary. The necessary diversity of tactics and strategy which is the inevitable consequence of the diversity of the situations (and a revolutionary incapable of grasping and exploiting the multifarious nature of reality would be a dogmatist, not a Marxist) nevertheless applies only where 'the internal factors' of a development are involved; the final break-through must always be the same and the basic lines of the strategy are constants.

Of course not even the current tactics of social democracy

consist of waiting for the development of capitalist contradictions to reach their peak and then undergo their sudden
change at that point. On the contrary, having recognized the
direction of a development, we base ourselves on it but in our
political struggle we then push its consequences to the extreme
and therein lies the essence of any revolutionary tactics.[133]

And further on: Social democracy

cannot and must not consist in waiting with arms crossed for
a 'revolutionary situation' to arise. On the contrary, it must
as always, *anticipate* developments and try to *speed them up*.
But that cannot be done by suddenly, out of the blue, at the
right or the wrong moment, issuing the order for a general
strike but above all by making plain to the widest possible
sections of the proletariat the inevitable coming of this revolutionary period, the *internal social* factors that lead up to it and
its political consequences.[134]

It is probably clear by now what we meant above when we
spoke of the 'what' and the 'how' as the difference between
revolutionary and opportunist strategy. In fact, Rosa Luxemburg
does not deny the validity of the demands that formed the so-
called minimum programme of the Social Democrats, the validity
of partial reforms and limited gains, any more than she questions
the value of the 'small routine task', because it is in fact in this
everyday action that she sees the source of the revolutionary
break-through. But whereas for the revisionists and, as we have
said, for the centrists and the self-styled 'orthodox' politicians,
these gains are valuable in themselves or, at the most, are stages
on the main road to socialism, for Rosa Luxemburg they also
offer dialectical proof of what the essence of capitalist society is
and its limitations. But in fact the two conceptions are completely
opposed if you look more closely at the matter, because in the
revolutionary conception all these gains, apart from their immediate value, have to serve the purpose of convincing the proletariat of the impossibility of changing its own situation in any
fundamental sense by means of such a struggle and the inevitability of a final seizure of political powers.[135] In other words the
struggles and gains cannot change the basic nature of imperialism
or its ineradicable tendencies; for that reason they make them
more obvious and thereby strengthen the will to fight and the
class consciousness of the workers, and by increasing social
tension, lead to the final crisis. The opportunists had practically
expunged this idea of final crisis from their conception of history

because it no longer fitted in with it, for if history is conceived of as a main road leading gradually to increasing higher stages of evolution, any talk of final crisis or catastrophe meant introducing an arbitrary element into the historical process from outside, contrary to the logic of the historical process, rather on the lines of Blanqui. And even these so-called orthodox thinkers who remained faithful to the idea of a final crisis in capitalist society were incapable of linking it to the day-to-day struggle precisely because they were unable to see the dialectical nature of the latter; for this reason, the famous collapse of capitalism seemed to them rather abstract, remote and mechanical almost like the execution of a death sentence pronounced by some transcendental force, a decree of fate or of history. In Rosa Luxemburg's conception, because of the importance that she attached to the day-to-day struggle as a way of constantly and consciously intervening in the historical process so as to make one trend of its development overcome the other, the revolutionary crisis is merely the final point in this process of development within which the tension between the two opposing poles has reached breaking point. 'Catastrophes' she points out 'are not in conflict with development but are a factor or phase in that development that only a petit bourgeois would find possible to conceive of as an imperceptible process, with various stages and degrees of development that glide into one another in a completely peaceful way.'[136]

In this matter of deeply diverging strategic approaches, it was only natural for Rosa Luxemburg to run up against the party's practical policy in every sphere. Engels had proposed three fields of activity for the proletarian struggle, the fields of economics, politics and ideology, but the last had now been practically abandoned, at least as an arena for the proletarian struggle to assert itself as an autonomous class and indeed it was the bourgeois ideologies which continually made further breaches in the social democratic position. There remained the economic struggle and the political struggle, the first of which was conceived as essentially a trade union struggle (the co-operative movement had no great prospects) and the second as a parliamentary struggle. Can these forms of action be considered, in themselves, as revolutionary, capable, as the revisionists maintained, of producing socialism from a capitalist society almost unbeknown to anyone by eliminating its contradictions little by little, making it milder and introducing fresh socialist elements into it by a gradual imperceptible process? Rosa Luxemburg disputed this attitude and showed that instead trade union and parliamentary activity inasmuch as they take place, by their very nature, inside the system and are thus subordinated to it, cannot by themselves fundamentally alter its essence.

Rosa Luxemburg's attitude towards the trade union problem had been plain ever since her article against Bernstein. In her attack on the revisionists' idea of giving the trade unions a major role in the struggle against capitalism (an increase in the level of wages compared to the amount of the gross national product and the progressive diminution of the latter compared to profits until the latter completely disappeared), she had remarked that the struggle of wages against profit was not an abstract one but that it took place on the concrete terrain of capitalist society and that as a result it could not, on its own, destroy capitalism's basic mechanism, the profit motive. She had shown that in the conditions then existing, the task of the unions was much more modest, albeit still essential. The trade unions, she wrote, cannot go outside the sphere of the organized sale of labour within capitalistic society but they can meanwhile effectively resist the trend towards the reduction of wages inherent in capitalist society and also achieve substantial improvements in working conditions; yet their field of possible action is limited by the conditions of the capitalist market on which the sale of labour takes place. The greatest possible success that they can achieve is thus to obtain the most favourable conditions compatible with capitalism and this cannot be achieved by rejecting the profit motive because that would bring the capitalist mechanism itself to a standstill. Since the conditions of the capitalist market are constantly changing, the trade unions will always have to work towards their goal, that is to say to endeavour to obtain the highest possible wage in the current market conditions; for this reason, its work is in a certain respect a labour of Sisyphus because it is never-ending and always needs repeating – although it is not a pointless labour since without it the worker's lot would become noticeably worse. The nature of trade union activity and the fact of its limited possibilities had a further political consequence, because this reminded the workers of the impossibility of freeing themselves from wage slavery unless they could destroy the existing conditions of labour and it also brought to their notice that the need to fight to bring down the capitalist system on the political field was a prerequisite for any real emancipation; in this sense the trade union struggle contributed to the formation of a political awareness and it was in this sense that Rosa Luxemburg referred to trade unionism as a school for socialism.

Both of these conceptions met strong resistance from trade unionists. They interpreted 'a labour of Sisyphus' as meaning 'pointless' and looked on it as a serious underestimation of trade union activity; they considered the formula 'trade unions as a school for socialism' as a denial of trade union autonomy and a theoretical justification of their subordination to the party. Rosa Luxemburg became at that time the black sheep of the trade unions and the constant subject of their attacks during the long drawn out disputes during the very first years of this century when they were trying to remove their own organization from any form of political leadership by the party.[137] The stronger the trade unions grew, the larger the number of their members and the better their organization the greater their authority became vis-à-vis the party: their superiority over the party in numbers and funds reached overwhelming proportions and this fact was bound to have an effect on their mutual relationship. This process was paralleled by another: the increasing importance of the unions strengthened the tendency in the labour movement to see as essential the day-to-day struggle and achievement of short term objectives rather than the ultimate goal of full-scale socialism. This soon led them to consider the highest aim of their activity as the strengthening of the organization, which thus became not a means in the struggle but its end, not an instrument of action but its purpose, an end that must in no circumstances be sacrificed or jeopardized. So as piecemeal reformism gradually prevailed, the organization eventually became an increasingly serious obstacle to action and struggle: the conservative attitude of trade union officialdom killed the class instinct and aggression of the masses. The revisionists and opportunists, who led the trade unions and – despite their revolutionary phrases – the party, reduced the struggle for socialism into everyday action, that is to say, to a parliamentary and trade union struggle and came to regard these two areas of activity as equally valid and independent manifestations of the labour movement. Hence there arose in practice the theory of the independence and equal rights of the party and the trade unions, a theory sanctioned by trade union congresses and party conferences and which received its seal of approval in an agreement which committed the leadership of the party to consult with the general committee of the trade unions before reaching decisions that might bind the workers in any matters regarded as the concern of the trade unions. Rosa Luxemburg raised vigorous opposition to this so-called parity of rights in the name of the unity of the labour movement on the grounds that it must not be split into two independent and separate sectors. Once again she employed the concept of totality to oppose the opportunists who were fragmenting the movement; the ultimate goal of the movement is a political one, the liberation of the workers from capitalist exploitation, and this aim can be pursued consciously only by the political organization of the proletariat, the socialist party which, as such, represents the totality of the movement. Trade union action is only one aspect of the total struggle and cannot be seen except in the context of the whole to which it must be subordinated. So equality of rights between trade union and party is an absurdity on the theoretical level, though, in German social democracy of the time, it had its practical justification in the fact that the party had abandoned the claim of being the expression of the conscious revolutionary will of the proletariat, a leader of all class activity, and reduced its own activity to pure Parliamentarianism, which is similarly an activity which can only take place in the framework of existing society; and by ceasing to be a unifying factor of the whole, it abandons, in practice, the ultimate goal.[138]

Naturally this subordination of the trade union to the party as understood by Rosa Luxemburg – although fitting into the concrete situation existing at the time – is not to be confused with the theory of the trade union as a mere 'conveyor belt' of the will or, worse still, of the orders of the party. Rosa Luxemburg never denied the autonomy of the trade union organization in its own sphere of organization, she merely considered that this activity must be regarded only as one aspect of a much wider activity, political in the broadest sense of the term, led by the party. Viewed thus, trade union activity is not entirely subsumed in its immediate achievements but has the task of creating a proletarian consciousness which, in a certain sense, is its culminating achievement. In fact, it is a question of bringing the workers into contact with the class limitations of present society to show them that any real liberation from the exploitation of which they are the victims is impossible within the existing framework of society and requires a fundamental social upheaval leading to the establishment of a socialist regime; so the trade union movement can make an effective contribution to the socialist struggle not so much by what it succeeds in obtaining, even if this is a considerable improvement, as by what it fails to obtain. This is only possible if the trade union remains within the sphere of the Marxist class struggle which was the reason of its strength and its superiority over other trade unions: to claim equal rights and so establish an autonomous 'trade union theory' of their own would mean depriving the trade unions of their main strength which is their Marxist doctrine, that is to say precisely that doctrine that gives the trade union the awareness of its function in the movement as a whole[139] and ultimately making it a cog in the bourgeois mechanism.

Similar considerations arise in the question of the parliamentary struggle when it is viewed not as a factor in the class struggle but as the form *par excellence* of the struggle for liberation, in accordance with the then fashionable theory that the progressive increase in the number of socialist votes would lead, effortlessly, to the consecration of socialism as a 'parliamentary party'. As we have said, Rosa Luxemburg strongly disliked any formulas claiming absolute validity and for this reason she did not exclude the possibility of a peaceful transition to socialism but she did exclude the possibility of turning this into a general principle and making it the result of a decision on the part of socialism, because the class struggle develops in accordance with certain specific historical conditions and must adapt itself concretely to such conditions: 'the problem of a revolution or a purely legal transition to socialism is not a tactical problem for social democracy but primarily a problem of "historical development";[140] yet it would be absurd to decide *a priori* to use legal means because 'what is presented to us as bourgeois legality is nothing but the power of the ruling class forced on us as an *a priori* norm.'[141] From this point of view, which admits the possibility of using both legal and illegal means in the struggle, parliamentary action is perfectly permissible and indeed is an effective instrument when its importance is not overrated. In the quiet periods of bourgeois society,

> social democracy's political struggle seems to be subsumed in the *parliamentary* struggle. However, the parliamentary struggle which is the counterpart of the trade union struggle is, like the latter, a struggle which takes place exclusively in the sphere of the bourgeois social order. It is, by its very nature, a work of political reform, just as the trade unions' is a work of economic reform. It consists of present political action just as the trade unions represent present economic action. Both of them are merely a phase, a stage in the development of the whole complex of the proletarian class struggle, whose ultimate goals go equally beyond both the parliamentary and the trade union struggle. So the parliamentary struggle also

stands in relation to social democracy's policies as a part to the whole, exactly like the struggle of the trade unions.[142]

If you allow the part to be considered as a whole, as was happening in the party in Baden at the time, you are subordinating yourself to bourgeois society. If Baden's attitude had been generally applied to the whole of Germany, 'social democracy would have simply ceased to exist.'[143] The watchword 'nothing but parliamentarianism' is in Marx's word 'parliamentary cretinism'.[144] But if you realize that 'chess moves and electoral strategies have no chance of altering historical facts'[145] and that the true power of the party lies in the awareness and solidarity of the masses, then Parliament is an area which the party must exploit to the full in its struggle.[146]

What we have said hitherto might seem absurd when one then learns that, in the German Social Democratic Party, Rosa Luxemburg was the leading light of the struggle for universal suffrage in Prussia (where there was still a three-tier voting system) as well as every other battle for the democratization of political institutions. Yet in fact there is nothing strange in this. Although Rosa Luxemburg did not regard Parliamentary government as a panacea for all ills, she was a firm believer in democratic values and in their importance in making the working masses, on whose shoulders the responsibility for furthering the historical process would fall, more aware and more mature. On the other hand, unlike her comrades in the party, she had no illusions as to the democratic nature of capitalist society nor about the natural process of democratic development that was supposed gradually to transfer power into the hands of the workers. On the contrary, she was amongst the first to recognize that capitalist society having now reached the imperialistic stage bore within itself the seeds of the destruction of democratic life and that it was thus necessary to wage war relentlessly against their opponents.

Analysing the historical trends of capitalist development and setting them against the trends of socialist development was, as we saw, the basis of Rosa Luxemburg's strategy. Once she had realized that far from favouring democracy, as her contemporaries amongst the Social Democrats believed, imperialism was by its very nature more likely to stifle it at birth, Rosa Luxemburg was bound to regard this as one of the basic contradictions of her time, since at the same time imperialism was drawing fresh masses of people into the productive process and thus bringing them face to face with the problem of their own social and

cultural betterment, a problem inseparably bound up with greater
democracy. This is why she was to behave so differently from the
others in the party. The ultraparliamentary leaders, thinking that
the storm would soon pass, relied on defensive tactics. They were
anxious not to inflame the situation but to act in a conciliatory
way so as to gain new support from among the moderate voters.
They did not want to engage in open battle and run the risk of
rousing reactionary ire which could jeopardize the fate of the
political and trade union organizations.[147] At the same time
Kautsky, the 'Marxist' and 'revolutionary', devised a new strategy
of attrition (*Ermattungsstrategie*)[148] or, to put it more plainly, did
nothing. It was only Rosa Luxemburg who took the lead in the
agitation to achieve universal suffrage and, to her party's horror,
spoke out in favour of a republic.

Ever since her pamphlet against Bernstein in 1898, Rosa Luxemburg had put forward this idea for the democratic struggle by the
proletariat.

> The steady progress towards democracy which seems to our
> revisionists as well as to the bourgeois liberals a fundamental
> law of the history of mankind or at least of modern history, if
> looked at more closely turns out to be a fantasy . . . So leaving
> aside any thought of a general historical law of the develop-
> ment of democracy, even in the present phase of bourgeois
> history we can see, even here, factors in the political situation
> that instead of leading to the realization of Bernstein's scheme
> are on the contrary going to lead to the abandonment by
> bourgeois society of previous democratic gains.[149]

Amongst the causes working in this direction, apart from the
fact that democratic institutions had largely exhausted their usefulness in helping the bourgeoisie in its rise to power, Rosa Luxemburg drew attention to the increasing burden of administration
and thus of bureaucracy in the State but, above all, to the development of imperialism and militarism: 'if international politics and
militarism are an *expanding* trend in the present phase, bourgeois
democracy must as a result be moving downwards',[150] (*international politics* being a synonym for imperialism); and, finally,
to the fear of the ruling class in face of the rise of the labour
movement. As a result,

> if democracy has become somewhat superfluous for the bour-
> geoisie, something of an obstacle, for the working classes on

the other hand it has become necessary and indispensable. Necessary first of all inasmuch as it offers the political forms (self-government, the right to vote, etc.) that will provide a base and support for the proletariat's task of transforming bourgeois society. But it is also indispensable because it is only through this, through its struggle on behalf of democracy, in the exercise of its democratic rights, that the proletariat can become aware of its own class interests and its own historic tasks. In short, democracy is indispensable not because it makes the seizure of power by the proletariat superfluous but on the contrary because it makes the seizure of power a *necessity* and at the same time the only *possibility*.[151]

And, a few years later, we find her writing:

If the social democratic parties in every country fight for a larger say in legislation and administration, for universal suffrage, compulsory free schooling and so on, it is not because these are only 'wonderful ideas' as good old Mr Limanovski would have said and because they are necessarily bound up with socialism but because all these democratic forms which are so necessary for the proletariat arise out of the development of bourgeois society and of capitalism. This is not altered by the fact that today the proletariat is fighting for the democratization of the bourgeois State, not side by side with the bourgeoisie, but against it. This fact proves that, at a certain advanced stage of development of class antagonism, the bourgeoisie ceases to be the representative of bourgeois development and its progressive element is taken over by the proletariat.[152]

In other words, whereas Bernstein had considered bourgeoisie democracy as a definitive achievement, indeed as the basic law of social development, Rosa Luxemburg rightly claimed that in the imperialistic phase, when the democratic function of the middle classes was finally exhausted, the proletariat should move into the forefront of the struggle for democracy, not in order to complete the bourgeois revolution but so as open up the new phase of the socialist revolution now that it had achieved ascendency in this sphere. After the 1905 Revolution in Russia, she saw this function of the proletariat with increasing clarity and thus rejected the Menshevik thesis that the socialist revolution should wait until the bourgeoisie had first completed the cycle of democratic revolution because this democratic bourgeois revolution had become impossible in the imperialist phase.[153]

But it is on the problem of war that Rosa Luxemburg's strategy has had a notable influence in the later development of the labour movement. Here Rosa Luxemburg introduced an important element of originality in her analysis of the development of capitalism and in identifying the type of catastrophe within that development towards which capitalism was heading. Both Marx and his successors had generally pointed to an economic crisis as the matrix of revolution and it was against this idea that Bernstein had battled. In her reply to him, Rosa Luxemburg stated that she did not consider it essential that an economic crisis would be the signal for the collapse of capitalism: 'Of course, there are reasons for regarding this collapse as resulting from a general and disastrous economic crisis but basically this is a marginal, not an essential factor.'[154] What was essential was that the development of capitalism necessarily contained elements of crisis and in the new imperialistic phase, this element could be war.[155] We have seen that Rosa Luxemburg started from the premise that imperialism was not a pathological state of the capitalist regime but a normal manifestation of the phase through which the world was passing; that behind the subtle moves of the international policies of the great imperialistic powers, economic trends were at work that were an 'historical necessity' for capitalism; that in times of peace this necessarily entails militarism and the armaments race and that all this will inevitably end in war. This theme of war had indeed often been raised at the congresses of the Internationale and the anarchists had constantly proposed that a general strike should take place when war was declared, a proposal that had been rejected as Utopian and unfeasible. On the other hand, the rightist elements among the socialists, for whom imperialism was a pathological state that could be remedied, deluded themselves that even war could be avoided by diplomatic measures and disarmament conferences and certainly did not think of war as providing a possible outlet for revolution.

Thus it was to Rosa Luxemburg's credit that she put the factor of militarism and war in the forefront of the considerations of the international movement as a potentially revolutionary factor. History was to prove her right both in the first Russian Revolution of 1905, which had arisen in the course of the Russo–Japanese War, and in the revolutions which accompanied or followed the two World Wars. Yet her campaign on this question dates from

1900, at the end of the decade that, as it were, marked the appearance of the imperialist phase.[156] At the party conference held in Mainz in September 1900, Rosa Luxemburg and her left-wing comrades expressly emphasized this point.[157] As a result she was appointed *rapporteur* for the Fourth Committee (international peace, militarism, abolition of standing armies) at the Paris Congress which immediately followed the Mainz Conference. In this capacity she pressed her point by emphasizing that this matter represented a new departure, that militarism had in fact become more widespread and more marked in the form of international policies based on imperialism and that bourgeois society had thereby entered into a new phase of its development; the development of the capitalist world had received fresh impetus but was thus hastening the fatal moment of its defeat.

Since this policy [she added] is beginning to dominate the entire home and foreign policies of the capitalist world, the socialists must organize their own policies to defend themselves against them. The time has come for the socialist party to take official cognisance of international politics; this is exactly what we wished to emphasize in our resolution. Still closer links between the proletarians of every country are necessary, not only to provide fresh impetus for our day-to-day struggle but also from the point of view of our ultimate goal. Citizens, at the beginning of the socialist movement, it was generally accepted that a major economic crisis would show the beginning of the end, yet it is increasingly more likely that it is rather a vast international political crisis which will toll the knell of capitalism. If as a result, citizens, the Marlborough of capitalism goes off to war, from which he will not return, if international policies lead to unexpected and incalculable conflicts and events then we must prepare ourselves urgently for the great role that sooner or later will fall to our lot.[158]

The famous resolution passed by the Stuttgart Congress in 1907 is merely a development of this premise. At Stuttgart, when it had become obvious to even the blindest of the members that the danger of war was approaching, militarism and international conflicts were the first and most important items on the agenda. The German delegates who set the tone of all international conferences were mainly drawn from the right and Bebel had tabled a motion in his normal centrist phraseology in which words were used in order to prevent any action. On the other side, three other resolutions had been tabled: one by Hervé, demanding a strike of the armed forces and a general uprising as an immediate answer to any declaration of war, from whichever side it might come, one by Guesde rejecting any idea of anti-war agitation inasmuch as militarism was inseparable from capitalism and would only be abolished by the wholesale victory of socialism, and finally, one by Jaurès and Vaillant which seemed the most realistic and sensible in its definition of the means to employ in the struggle against militarism. Rosa Luxemburg, who represented Poland's Social Democrats at the Congress, was put on the sub-committee set up to work out a compromise motion to put before the Congress; this was at Lenin's suggestion who had her nominated by the Russian Social Democratic Party for the purpose. As the representative of two parties, the Russian and the Polish, she put forward an amendment to Bebel's motion that was later to become the platform for Lenin's own struggle during the First World War. The amendment was related to the Paris Congress report because it ended with the statement that the socialist parties must use the political and economic crises caused by war to stir up the masses of the people as energetically as possible so as to throw off the capitalist yoke; this would be possible only by constantly intensifying the struggle against militarism and imperialism both before the war and as the danger became more threatening, using the most vigorous methods that the situation allowed. In defending this amendment, which was passed, she opposed the German delegates Bebel and von Vollmar, who had said, 'We were in no position to do anything more than we had previously done. But the Russian Revolution has not only come about as a result of the war but has also contributed to ending it. The Tsarist regime would otherwise certainly have continued to fight on. For us the dialectics of history do not mean standing with folded arms until ripe fruit falls into our hands. I am a convinced supporter of Marxism and this is why I consider it very dangerous to allow Marx's ideas to be forced into a rigid fatalistic mould which can only give rise to such excessive reaction as Hervé's.'[159]

Stuttgart was a turning point in the anti-war struggle because Rosa Luxemburg's amendment[160] gave a new orientation to the Marxist attitude, one that was confirmed by the next international Congresses, especially the one in Basle in 1912.[161] Yet Rosa Luxemburg knew that the confirmation of a principle has little value unless it is put into action; it is not possible to use war to trigger off revolution unless war has been opposed a long time in advance. If the dialectical contradiction between the 'historical necessity' of imperialism and of socialism is inherent in every moment of the development of history, when each moment contains potentially two contradictory sorts of future, the possibility of one of them prevailing rather than the other depends on *how* the opposing social forces succeed in linking each separate moment to the changing historical facts. On the one hand, having recognized militarism and war as two aspects of the historical necessity of imperialism, Rosa Luxemburg knew that only the labour movement could take over the defence of peace[162] and so she saw the battle against militarism and the forthcoming war as a class need of the proletariat, the more so as the coming war was in her eyes the matrix of the political crisis that would be able to produce the revolutionary impetus to bring about the collapse of capitalist society. Since, however, every revolution relies on the broad participation of conscious masses of people and since this awareness can only be acquired by experience and struggle, the commitment to antimilitarism becomes a necessary condition in preparing revolution; without such preparation the moment of crisis would still come but would find the proletariat unprepared for its task, as in fact happened. This was all the truer because on this question Rosa Luxemburg followed Engels in believing that the revolution would finally triumph not as the result of a victory achieved by the people under arms over the army but when the armed forces themselves came over to the side of the people. But this required an awareness and a political maturity amongst the soldiers which would free them from the system of obedience unto death which had been imposed on them by military discipline and training. So to achieve this purpose a long period of education was necessary which above all had to appeal to young people: anti-militarist propaganda ought to heal the divorce between the army and the people by undermining obedience to those in authority in the minds of the people and replacing it by the angry desire to fight the resulting oppression as well as the danger of war. But the socialists who set out to be conciliatory, to smooth over conflicts and collaborate with the enemy, to justify its attitudes as being 'democratic' or 'peaceful', the socialists who hope to gain peace or achieve democracy by collaborating with the forces of imperialism are an objective obstacle to the socialist solution, and thus an objective support for imperialism.[163] 'By voting for the military estimates and accepting a civil truce' social democracy 'is using every means to avoid creating an economic and political crisis, and arousing the masses as a result of the war'[164] wrote Rosa Luxemburg during the war itself. And the German Social Democrats were certainly responsible to a large extent when, in the course of the revolutionary crisis following the war, not only was every socialist solution blocked but the class domination of imperialist capitalism was left almost intact so that it could take its revenge with Hitler a few years later.

So Rosa Luxemburg's strategy was completely opposed to the official party line, particularly after 1905. She was certain that a world war was imminent, she could see that the closer imperialism drew to its final trial of strength, the greater was its need to stifle the democratic way of life and she could thus recognize on the principal battle fronts the elements of acute crisis which could have offered a powerful impetus for a revolutionary solution. But a revolution not only requires the existence of the objective conditions that make it possible but also active participation and thus a subjective preparation of the masses. How could this preparation, which should have been one of the Social Democrats' main tasks, be pursued? For Rosa Luxemburg as for Marx, awareness comes from practical experience and class-consciousness from class struggle: pamphlets and propagandist speeches alone would never be enough without the direct experience of the masses. Yet the direct experience of the masses requires in its turn to be guided and led by social democracy so as to grasp the essentially contradictory nature of present society, that is to say to rise above the chance circumstance, the partial objective and the day-to-day struggle to an overall view of society, to recognize in every conflict the class barriers that constitute the insuperable obstacle to eliminating the deeper causes of the conflict itself within the framework of present society.[165] Here again there is the reference to the idea of totality, the view of the future as immanent in the present, the permanent link between the day-to-day struggle and the ultimate goal. Thus it is the party's task not only to seize every opportunity to fight, every possibility of mobilizing the masses but also to explore the conditions of the struggle as thoroughly as possible and to exacerbate the conflicts because not only will this develop the awareness of the masses but it will prepare for the revolutionary crisis and bring it nearer, that is to say transform what, as we saw, are merely immanent trends in the development of society into real developments and turn the historical necessity of the socialist revolution into an historical reality.

All this cannot, of course, be brought about artificially; without real contradiction or real social tension, the masses will not be driven to struggle and if there is no spontaneous impulse from the masses, the party slogans will not suffice by themselves. Yet real contradictions are not lacking in capitalist society, indeed they are an essential factor of that society. The object of strategy and above all of tactics must be from time to time to select the most valid motives, discover tensions, even when they are hidden, recognize imbalances and exploit every pretext. And in addition they must endeavour to combine these diverse forces into one unified political movement that is plainly directed towards the most advanced objective possible at the time, the one that can offer a common point of reference for the various existing struggles; only in this way can one avoid being hemmed into a restricted and fragmentary area (which as such is bound to remain within the framework of the present society) and direct the workers' struggle along socialist lines. Moreover, society's contradictions must not be regarded as being merely a crude fact, purely objective and independent of the presence and the action of the masses, because the historical process is always the fruit of a mutual interaction of objective and subjective factors; in the last analysis the acuteness and thus the revolutionary potential of capitalist contradictions is an indication of the degree of awareness and pugnacity of the workers.

This was in Rosa Luxemburg's mind from the beginning of her activity and we find it illustrated in the first report she drew up for the International Congress in Zürich on the situation in Poland.[166] From this point of view her analysis of the Russian Revolution of 1905 in her short work on the general strike is particularly successful and suggestive. The close unity of the political and the economic struggle – two aspects of the same class struggle – the creative power of action and the possibility of creating fresh waves of it, the swift ripening of awareness under the fire of battle and the growth of new powers of organization by reason of the experiences of the struggle itself, are all manifestly plain in Rosa Luxemburg's account, from which there also clearly emerges a strategy exploiting every possibility of struggle by creating or cultivating in every fight an awareness of more advanced aims and broader objectives in order to combine all the aspirations of the people into a coherent whole. And it is the great value of this experience and certainly not any mere mechanical repetition of acts which she strove to make part of the consciousness of the proletariat of the west.

During these years she placed the main emphasis of her activity

in Germany on agitating against militarism and in favour of
universal suffrage, because she considered that it was here that
imperialism was most threatening and aggressive and that the
public should concentrate on reacting on these two points. But
she never intended turning this into agitation for the sake of it.
In every one of her controversies during these years two constant
motives appear again and again: first the need to keep the proletariat constantly on the offensive, never letting any movement
die down once it had been aroused, never allowing the accumulated potential of any struggle to become dispersed and secondly
the need to break through the barriers of sectarianism, to urge
the workers on in their will to struggle towards common political
objectives.[167] Thus she criticized the party and its official organ
Vorwärts for keeping separate the two principal causes of agitation of the time, the agitation for universal suffrage and the agitation against unemployment (a fine example of Kautsky's sort of
strategy of attrition!) instead of linking the demand for bread and
for work with the demand for the vote;[168] thus during the electoral
campaign of 1911 she protested against the party directive restricting the electoral campaign to questions of home policy, taxes
and social legislation.

> But financial policy, the domination of the Junkers, the stand-
> still in social reform are all organically linked with militarism,
> naval rearmament, colonial policy, personal rule and its foreign
> policy. Any artificial separation of these matters can only lead
> to an incomplete and one-sided picture of our political situa-
> tion. In the Reichstag elections our main task is to spread the
> light of socialism but this cannot be done if we only criticize
> Germany's home policies; we must point out our main links
> with other countries, the progress of capitalist domination in
> every continent, the blatant anarchy visible everywhere, and
> the predominant part played by colonial policy and interna-
> tional politics in this whole process.[169]

And attacking the patient and soporific theory of attrition she
wrote:

> Not attrition but a fight all along the line; that is what we
> need. Not the consoling hope of revenge at the ballot boxes in
> eighteen months' time but a good hard blow now, quickly, and
> again and again.[170]

The only possible unifying aim of all these fights was the

battle against imperialism which summed up the essence of all
the contradictions in society:

> Militarism and imperialism are at the moment the central
> problems of our political life and the key to the political
> situation lies there and not in any question of industrial re-
> sponsibility or any other purely parliamentary demands.[171]

But the visible support for these imperial policies and the
focus of all the forces of reaction is the monarchy.

> Over the last quarter of a century and increasingly so with
> every passing year the semi-feudal monarchy with its personal
> form of government has undoubtedly provided the basis for
> militarism, the driving force behind the policy of naval
> rearmament, the guiding spirit behind imperialist ventures,
> just as it provides support for the Junkers in Prussia and the
> bulwark for the predominance of Prussia's political backward-
> ness throughout Germany: it is thus as it were the sworn
> personal enemy of the German working class and social
> democracy. So the watchword of republicanism in Germany
> is now infinitely more than a beautiful dream of a democratic
> people's State or abstract political doctrinairism, it is a practical
> war cry against militarism, navalism,[172] colonial policy,
> imperialism, the domination of the Junkers and the prussifica-
> tion of Germany, it is nothing but a consequence and a drastic
> synthesis of our day-to-day fight against all these partial aspects
> of the current reaction.[173]

For Rosa Luxemburg, a drastic synthesis of all the separate
struggles was the melting pot in which all the energies of the
working classes would fuse and draw into the struggle forces that
official party policy and the trade union organizations were holding at arm's length and in particular the unorganized masses who
frightened the leaders, concerned at all costs to preserve order
and discipline in the agitations which they fostered.[174] And in this
melting pot Rosa Luxemburg also hoped to weld into one the
proletarians in their overalls with the proletarians in uniform;
the latter 'are merely part of the working class population and if
this class can achieve the necessary awareness of the fact that
war is wrong and harmful to the people, then even soldiers will
understand of their own accord without any injunction on our
part what they have to do in any particular case.'[175] If only the
Social Democratic Party itself does not check their impetus, it can
be possible to form a common front of all the workers against

'the prevailing sabre-rattling spirit of adventure' that threatens international peace and by creating a state of siege militates against public security and personal rights, that even jeopardizes universal suffrage and the right to form associations.[176]

It is common knowledge that the German Social Democrats in fact decided to hold back the masses by treating Rosa Luxemburg's realistic prohecies as fancies. And in so doing they actively helped the imperialists to unleash the First World War. The picture which we have tried to give of Rosa Luxemburg's strategy would however be incomplete unless we emphasized that, in her view, the proletariat's radical opposition to bourgeois society on behalf of socialism was to give the proletariat not only political but cultural autonomy.

> Very soon . . . socialism's efforts to save civilization from Prussian feudal reaction will become increasingly vigorous as a direct result of the liquidation of revisionism. Because the socialist movement's close connection with intellectual progress does not stem from the efforts of bourgeois who have come over to socialism but from the rise of the masses of the proletariat. This connection is based not on any affinity of our movement with bourgeois society but from its opposition to that society. Its *raison d'être* is the ultimate goal of socialism to give back all the civilized values to the whole of mankind. And the more the proletarian nature of social democracy comes to the fore, the greater the possibility that German civilization will be saved from its friends east of the Elbe and Germany itself will escape from the sort of Chinese ossification wished on it by the conservatives.[177]

Revolution

*The difficulties of the task do not lie in the strength
of our opponents or the resistance of bourgeois
society. The difficulties lie in the proletariat itself,
in its lack of maturity or rather in the lack of
maturity of its leaders, of the socialist parties.*

ROSA LUXEMBURG

ROSA LUXEMBURG's method and strategy which we have been
describing hitherto are concerned in general with the class
struggle being fought within the framework of capitalist society
with the aim of preparing and hastening the moment of the
decisive clash. Let us now see how this strategy fits into the
course of the actual revolutionary struggle.

We have already seen that one of Rosa Luxemburg's most
important contributions to revolutionary theory lay in the link
she established between revolution and war rather than revolution and crisis. Another important aspect of her thought to which
we drew attention was her endeavour to realize a synthesis
between the Russian and the western experience : the latter was
able to provide an example of a working class which, because it
was more mature and participated more directly in the political
struggle possessed the necessary qualities to become a ruling
class; on the other hand the former, offered an example of a more
aggressive spirit, a more powerful revolutionary drive. It was less
closely integrated into a capitalist State and thus possessed a
greater possibility of making a radical break with the system. In
other words, although she recognized that the German working
classes and their party had a leading role through their political
ability to provide a future government and through their militant
methods adapted to an advanced capitalist society, Rosa Luxemburg was inclined to expect any revolutionary impulse to come
from Russia. In her stubborn controversies with the Polish
Socialist Party whose programme included amongst its objectives
the re-establishment of a Polish State and renewed contact with
the western socialists who supported it in the name of their

long-standing aversions to the Tsarist regime, she had always asserted that at this point of time, it was a mistake to see Russia as a bulwark of reaction because the seeds of revolution were now ripening in the Russian masses and that these could be most fruitful.[178]

In view of these two assumptions it was thus only natural that, as leader of the Polish Social Democrats, she fought against the Russo–Japanese War and tried to exploit it for revolutionary purposes, as did the Russian Bolsheviks with whom a marked rapprochement took place at that time.[179] In her interpretation of the significance of the 1905 Revolution she found herself in conflict with all the systematic pseudo-Marxists who saw the history of every country as a regular series of historical phases that the more advanced countries had already been through and for that reason spoke in terms of a democratic bourgeois revolution that was supposed to mark the transition from a semi-feudal, absolutist regime to a capitalist, parliamentary one. With her capacity for close analysis of different situations and her concern to place every event in the totality of all its relationships, Rosa Luxemburg was bound to realize that the revolution was taking place in a country where a working class and a socialist party already existed and where on the other hand the bourgeoisie was relatively weak and timid and more inclined to compromise with the aristocracy; and this could not fail to make that revolution profoundly different from the western bourgeois revolutions. That is to say that in Russia there was an historical overlapping of conditions with the proletariat and the Social Democrats as protagonists in a revolution before the bourgeoisie had even completed its historical cycle, even before it had been able to come into power.[180] This interpretation destroyed the rigidly scholastic idea of a single united course of history valid for all countries, where socialist revolution comes at the end of the development of capitalism, when society has been entirely reduced to a purely capitalist form with a clear break between a strongly concentrated capitalism and an over-whelming majority of wage-earners organized by the Social Democrats. On the other hand, through this interpretation Lenin's later theory of the weakest link was introduced, a theory which had incidentally to some extent been anticipated by Marx, in the sense that, because of this overlapping of conditions, the pro-letariat of a backward country, where capitalism and the power of the State were weaker, could more easily succeed.

The present revolution thus realizes in the special circumstances of absolutist Russia, the general consequences of the development of international capitalism as well and appears not so much as a successor to the bourgeois revolutions of old as the forerunner of a new series of proletarian revolutions in the west. The most backward country, just because it has been so unpardonably late in producing its bourgeois revolution, can show the proletariat ways and means for further class struggle both in Germany and the most advanced capitalist countries.[181]

This thesis of Rosa Luxemburg's is in marked contrast to that of the Mensheviks, who thought that Russia must on the contrary pass through every phase of development that had occurred in advanced countries and must therefore experience a democratic bourgeois revolution and then a period of parliamentary struggle, etc., before there could be any talk of a socialist revolution. In this conception the labour movement is relegated to a subordinate position; the idea was to help the bourgeoisie to achieve power in order to make the full expansion of capitalism possible and out of this the labour movement would emerge with increased strength.

For Rosa Luxemburg, as for the socialist left in general, it was on the contrary for the proletariat to lead the revolutionary struggle because it was the only class capable of waging a struggle (bourgeois capitalism and the petty bourgeoisie were too weak and moreover too much inclined to compromise with the aristocracy), even although it was not yet powerful enough to set up a socialist government since external conditions did not permit it.

If we reach the conclusion that in the present revolution the bourgeoisie is not playing and cannot play the leading part in the liberation movement, that the essence of its politics makes it counterrevolutionary, if as a result we state that the proletariat must no longer consider itself as an auxiliary force to support liberalism but as the vanguard of the revolutionary movement which, while naturally taking account of other classes in drawing up its policies, yet bases them exclusively on its own class interests and responsibilities, if we say that the proletariat's role is not just to help the bourgeoisie into the saddle but to establish its own independent policy – if we can say all this then it seems clear that any proletariat which has achieved real awareness must exploit every revolutionary movement among the people and subordinate it to their control and their class politics.[183]

These words come from her attack on the Mensheviks during the London Congress of the Social Democratic Labour Party of Russia in 1907.

'To exploit every revolution among the people and subordinate it to their control and their class politics' : this also raises the question of the relation between the proletariat and the peasants. Rosa Luxemburg firmly rejected the Mensheviks' theory according to which the peasants as a whole were a reactionary class but she also refused to accept the opposite thesis that they would actively support the socialist revolution until the end. Her position and that of her party was that a distinction must be made between a potentially revolutionary section (day labourers and poor peasants) and a potentially reactionary section (moderately prosperous and rich farmers) and that nevertheless the peasants as soon as they had come into possession of some land would be an obstacle to the further development of the struggles for socialism. For this reason she believed that the working class should never abandon its predominant role or its leadership in the struggle and she replaced Lenin's formula of 'democratic revolutionary dictatorship of the proletariat and the peasants' by her own formula of 'revolutionary dictatorship of the proletariat supported by the peasants'.

But although the proletariat must maintain its leadership of the revolution until Tsarism has been crushed and perhaps until it has taken over power, it would not be capable of retaining power, on the one hand because of the manifold tasks awaiting it,[184] on the other because of the international situation.[185] None the less the Russian proletariat, even if unsuccessful, was beginning a fresh chapter of history, that of the socialist revolution and this was important for two reasons. First of all for Russia itself where, even if defeated, the revolution would create a situation making it impossible for the old regime to continue in power unchanged, while the bourgeoisie would not be able to consolidate its own power. For this reason, as she later wrote, the defeat in 1906 was not a failure but merely the natural conclusion of the first chapter which would be followed by others with the inevitability of a law of nature.[186] The 1917 Revolution proved her right.

At the same time, in an international situation where everything was stagnating, the Russian Revolution opened up the question of revolution in Germany, that is to say the country with the largest socialist party. In this alliance between the Russian and the German proletariat of which she was very conscious, the former was clearly indebted to the latter for Marxist theory, for the experience of the class struggle and generally everything necessary to create and develop a social democratic party. On the other hand the Russian proletariat could teach its Western counterpart 'new ways and means of fighting' and these could help future revolutionary action. The close unity of the international struggle for the proletariat was at the centre of Rosa Luxemburg's efforts as a socialist politician belonging to two parties, one of which was active within the frontiers of the Tsarist empire, the other in Germany; this was, so to speak, her revolutionary vocation.[187]

The leaders of the German Social Democratic Party who were so proud of their powerful organization and at the same time so dogmatically attached to the idea of the single evolution of capitalism in every country, were naturally unable to accept the idea that a Russian proletariat was in the forefront of the socialist revolution and indeed was leading the German proletariat and German social democracy. They were bound to be perturbed by a passage such as the following written by Rosa Luxemburg:

> Thus even regarded in this way it seems completely false to look at the Russian Revolution from a distance as a splendid example, something specifically Russian and at best merely admire the heroism of those taking part in the struggle, that is to say, the outward trappings of the struggle. It is much more important for the German workers to learn to look at the Russian Revolution as *their own business*, not only as a matter of international class solidarity with the Russian proletariat but above all as a *chapter in their own social and political history*. Those trade union leaders and parliamentarians who consider the German proletariat as 'too weak' and conditions in Germany as not yet ripe for revolutionary struggle by the masses have obviously no idea that the maturity of Germany's class attitudes and the power of the proletariat are not to be measured by German trade unions' statistics or by electoral statistics but by the events of the Russian Revolution. Just as the degree of maturity of class contradictions in France under the July Monarchy and in the fighting in June was mirrored in the course and in the fiasco of the March Revolution in Germany, so the degree of maturity of the class conflict in Germany is mirrored in the events and in the strength of the

Russian Revolution. And while the bureaucrats in the German labour movement are rummaging about in the drawers of their offices to find proof of their strength and maturity they fail to realize that what they are looking for is being made historically manifest under their very noses, because considered historically the Russian Revolution is a reflection of the power and maturity of the international labour movement, that is, primarily, of the German labour movement.[188]

Unfortunately it was not only the party officials who rejected these ideas but even her radical friends, including Kautsky himself who at that time had not officially gone over to centrism. From this moment onwards, after these controversies the friendly and hitherto extremely close relationship between Rosa Luxemburg and Kautsky begins to cool until in 1910 open war was declared between the two.[189]

Was Rosa Luxemburg's vision a Utopian or realistic one? Any reply to this question requires, in our view, an examination both of the political conditions in Germany during this period as well as of the methods Rosa Luxemburg proposed to carry on the struggle and here she introduces the two most hotly debated aspects of her thought, her theory of the general strike and of the relationship between class and party as well as her so-called theory of 'spontaneity'.

Nothing would be more stupid in considering whether conditions were ripe for revolution in Germany than to cling blindly to historical data. If in fact the occurrence of an event proves that it was historically possible (thus for example the success of the Bolshevik revolution in 1917 proved that Rosa Luxemburg's predictions as to the developments that would follow after the first revolutionary act in 1905 were well founded), it cannot be stated with equal certainty that its non-occurrence is proof of its historical impossibility because it is always conceivable that a different attitude on the part of the protagonists would have brought other events to fruition. In this case, there is nothing to justify our assertion that the revolution would have failed if Rosa Luxemburg's revolutionary theses had been adopted by the leaders of the German Social Democratic Party. Amongst the factors leading to the success of a revolution, the attitude of the political leaders of the revolutionary party is undoubtedly one of the most important but if, instead of leading the revolution, this party makes every effort to prevent it or to stifle it, it is difficult to believe in the success of a revolution. So it would be tautologous to say that the German Social Democrat leaders were right in rejecting Rosa Luxemburg's political prognostications because their rejection made it impossible to verify their truth. So the argument is rather a complicated one and we shall restrict ourselves to mentioning only a few of the points necessary to reach a judgement.

Above all it must not be forgotten that for Rosa Luxemburg revolution is not an unheralded settlement of accounts between the proletariat and capitalism but a fact in the course of capitalist development which occurs whenever the contradictions and tensions produced by this development have reached their climax. As the struggle grows, the maximum tension is produced; the seizure of power by the proletariat, that is to say the triumph of the socialist revolution, is not to be regarded as an act in a single moment of time, as a final violent collision, but as the con-clusion of a revolutionary process. She rightly pointed out that 'the old belief in violent revolution as the *sole* method of con-ducting the class struggle and as the means of creating a socialist system *at all times*'[190] had been set aside by social democracy. In reality, 'the seizure of power by the working classes can only be the end result'[191] of a more or less lengthy period of normal day-to-day struggle. 'For this reason this task can also not be achieved at one blow but similarly over a long period of gigantic social struggle'.[192] And even in the last few days before her death in the blaze of revolution, when she regarded the realization of socialism as the current task, she did not abandon her conception of the seizure of power as a process: at the foundation of the Communist Party, she spoke these words: 'So the seizure of power is to be a continuous and not a single process, as we thrust into the bour-geois State until we have occupied every post and defend them tooth and nail.'[193]

So after 1905, if Rosa Luxemburg spoke of the possibility of a socialist revolution in Germany, she was not in any way thinking of a sudden outbreak of revolution but of growing tension and struggle, the result of which might be the seizure of power. There was certainly no lack of opportunities for tension and struggle: apart from militarism and the right to vote which we have already mentioned, the economic situation also offered great possibilities. In her article on the general strike Rosa Luxemburg drew attention to the real economic condition of the German workers, many of whom were working under conditions of gross exploitation. It would thus not have been difficult to launch them into downright battles, as was proved indeed on two occasions

during this period, in 1905 and 1910. The second occasion
coincided with an agitation for the right to vote in Prussia, an
agitation that reached alarming proportions for the government,
although the trade union party leaders always tried to restrain the
masses. Even the struggle against militarism achieved great popularity, as for example in the Zabern case.[194] According to Rosenberg, the war caught the German people in an untenable and
intolerable situation in its home affairs. Between 1908 and 1914
the contrast between the ruling aristocracy and the masses of the
people had become increasingly sharp. Events such as the 'Daily
Telegraph affair', the 1912 elections and the Zabern dispute did
not, of course, mean revolution but they were typical of a revolutionary epoch. Had the 1914 War not broken out, the conflicts
between the Kaiser's government and the great majority of the
German people would have continued to grow until a directly
revolutionary situation would have arisen. So the outbreak of war
at first bridged the gulf existing in home affairs without, however,
eliminating it.[195] And Bartel stated: 'In 1914 German imperialism
tried to find the solution of its internal and external conflicts in
war.'[196]

As for the mood of the masses, it would not be difficult to produce document after document to prove that where revolutionary
fighting spirit was concerned they were far ahead of their official
leaders. Writing about the immediate pre-war period, Clara
Zetkin said:

> In fact, large masses of the proletariat were burning to fight
> militarism and imperialism. Insofar as their class consciousness
> had not yet clearly recognized the mortal enemy, their healthy
> class feeling was able to smell him out instinctively.[167]

In 1914 when Rosa Luxemburg was condemned by a Frankfurt
court for incitement to disobedience in the army, an enormous
wave of resentment ran through the masses, but there was an even
greater one when another case against her was announced because
she had denounced the ill-treatment of soldiers; according to Clara
Zetkin's report, more than 3,000 ill-treated soldiers offered to give
evidence so that the authorities had to drop the case.[198] And it is
significant that at a party meeting – in a party inured to the
strictest discipline towards its leaders and ruled with a rod of
iron by Ebert and Scheidemann – Rosa Luxemburg succeeded in
having a resolution passed by a large majority in the plenary
session of the Berlin organization calling on all members of the
party to convince the workers that only the strongest pressure of

the will of the people, only a general strike, would be able to bring equal voting rights in Prussia.[199] The mass demonstrations against the threat of war on 28 July 1914 were further confirmation of this mental attitude which would have developed had it not been prevented by decision of the leaders. If the military dictatorship set up during the war succeeded in stifling – though not completely preventing – further demonstrations, to prove the feelings of the masses on the eve of the war it may suffice to quote Kautsky as an unimpeachable witness, writing in connection with the recent release from prison of Liebknecht who had been detained during the war. 'No monarch was ever more enthusiastically received in Berlin by a gigantic mass of people as Liebknecht on his arrival at the Anhalter railway station.'[200] It is therefore permissible to ask what would have happened had the Social Democratic Party followed Rosa Luxemburg's strategy to the full, that is to say if, instead of smoothing things over, stifling reactions, keeping quiet themselves and making sure the masses kept quiet too, it had set about exacerbating conflicts and strengthening the will to fight. Certainly class consciousness, which Marx considered always an antagonistic consciousness nourished on direct experience of the struggle and the clear awareness of the existence of basic contradictions, would have emerged stronger as a result. Any strengthening of class consciousness would in turn have made social democracy more attractive and encouraged new masses to join in the struggle, swept along by the power and contagious example of the fighting spirit which was preached so frequently and so successfully by Rosa Luxemburg. Certainly no one would have been more opposed to agitation on a large scale planned and executed in cold blood round a table than Rosa Luxemburg, and no one knew better than she that without definite conditions, that is to say lively social contradictions and psychological tensions as well as the resulting spontaneous participation of the masses, any agitation is doomed to failure. Yet if these conditions exist and these tensions are operative, if the masses feel the instinctive urge to action, very little will suffice to unleash a storm. And it is in just such cases that a political battle can spark off a series of economic claims of which the most neglected and least organized sections of the community or forces (eg the army) subjected to particular pressures had hitherto been unaware; and we have already emphasized that Rosa Luxemburg relied precisely on these sections and these forces and not only on the proletariat in the narrow sense of the word.

The specific form of struggle which she advocated, for example in connection with the 1905 Russian Revolution, was the general strike. This measure had long been discussed in the labour movement and it was also a point of contention between Marxists and anarchists. For the latter the general strike was a revolutionary act that would put paid to capitalist society. Engels' retort was that however strong they might be, in order to start a general strike on their own and to be able to continue it until the collapse of capitalist society, the workers would have to be strong enough to seize power without needing to rely on recourse to a general strike. Engels' opposing view clearly prevailed over that of the anarchists at the Second Internationale at the Brussels Congress of 1891, a motion proposing the general strike in case of war was rejected. But while the congresses merely talked about it, the general strike was in fact successfully used by the Belgium workers in their struggle to obtain universal suffrage. So the Zürich Congress of 1893 reopened the discussion and the committee approved a resolution prepared by Kautsky which, while condemning the anarchists' conception of the general strike, recognized that in certain economic and political circumstances it could be an effective weapon, provided that the political and trade union organization of the working classes was a strong one. Thereafter the general strike was actually used or at least considered in connection with the struggle for universal suffrage in various countries.

In Germany, Bernstein[202] and Parvus[203] both advocated it but the majority was against them. In the massive Belgian strike of 1902, Rosa Luxemburg also made an effective contribution to the debate: she showed how abstract were those (the anarchists) who supported the general strike absolutely as the supreme, universally valid weapon and thus failed to take account '*of the local conditions existing at the time, of the concrete political state of the class struggle in every country* and at the same time of the organic link between the definitive struggle of socialism with the day-to-day struggles of the proletariat, *its gradual enlightenment and organization*'.[204] In her view, it was rather a question of recognizing the concrete possibility of a general strike when the objective conditions demanded it and the mass basis had been provided. Mehring,[205] Hilferding,[206] Eckstein[207] and Kautsky[208] all made their contribution to the debate, with the latter adopting a basically cautious attitude since he thought the general strike should be used only in the final decisive battle to seize power but not as a means to achieve isolated successes, such as the right to vote or to form associations. Since the struggle for political power was not on the cards for the moment neither was a general strike. A similar attitude was adopted by the majority of the International Socialist Congress of 1904 in Amsterdam which passed a resolution stating that the general strike could only be used as a last resort to bring about important social changes or to oppose reactionary attacks against workers' 'rights' and warning that organization and discipline were essential prerequisites for success. The congress had barely ended before the outbreak of the 1904 general strike in Italy, which had great repercussions throughout Europe.[209]

The German Social Democratic Party was basically always opposed to a general strike and Kautsky's cautious and subtle formulas had successfully hidden this fact beneath an apparent theoretical recognition hedged round with conditions.[210] Parvus was the only person to speak out openly in favour while Friedeberg's[211] unambiguous attitude was inspired by anarchism. The overwhelming majority of the German Social Democratic Party remained true to Ignaz Auer's formula: 'General strike, general madness.' As often happens, however, events led to a renewed discussion of a problem that had to be solved. After the years of economic prosperity and increasing affluence which had favoured the rise of revisionism, German workers were faced by fresh problems: wages failed to keep pace with the increasing cost of living and the wage earners' share in the gross national product fell during those years proportionately more than in other European countries. The trade union struggle became keener: in 1903–4 there was the big textile workers' strike in Crimmitschau and in 1905 the colossal miners' strike in the Rhur broke out. It began on 7 January; by the 17th, 155,000 miners had come out and on the 20th they had been joined by a further 14,000 in Upper Silesia. The 22nd was the day of the blood bath at St Petersburg and this had an electrifying effect on the German workers – by 9 February out of a total of 268,000 miners in Germany, 220,000 were on strike. Unfortunately, however, it had quite the opposite effect on the trade union leaders. The Christian trade unions ended the strike and persuaded the others to do the same. All the same, it was a strike of an unprecedented magnitude for Germany at that time. Later on, particularly important strikes were that of the construction workers in Rhineland-Westphalia, that of the textile industry in Saxony-Thuringia and the strike in the Berlin electrical industry. The number of workers taking part in militant industrial action (strikes and lock-outs) which was 55,713 (964,317 days) in 1902, rose to 121,593 (2,622,232 days) in 1903, 135,957 (2,160,154 days) in 1904 and in 1905, under the influence of the events in Russia, it rose steeply to 507,964 workers and a good 7,362,802 days of conflict. The general strike which social democracy had always rejected in practice and which the Bremen Congress formally buried in 1904 when it rejected a motion of Karl Liebknecht and Clara Zetkin that it should be tried out, was ceasing to be the subject of purely academic discussion.

Rosa Luxemburg had hitherto taken little part in the discussion, for the good reason that it seemed to have little immediate connection with the actual state of affairs in Germany; her intervention in the debate which we mentioned was a commentary on the Belgian general strike. Theoretically her position had not basically changed: she condemned the general strike as conceived by the anarchists as an abstract recipe for revolution but neither did she agree with those who accepted it for predetermined aims (eg as a defence against attacks on the right to vote) and saw it as a mass action, relying only on organization and discipline, which could thus be switched on and off as required. The Russian Revolution which had produced an impressive series of general strikes had clearly proved that striking was a weapon which presupposed, in a sense, a revolutionary situation and could thus not be produced artificially. On the one hand, strong social and political tension as an objective prerequisite and on the other hand, subjectively, a high degree of participation by the masses which cannot be produced by organization and discipline alone but is essentially linked with the existing tension and can thus be achieved by unorganized masses. 'To be frank,' Rosa Luxemburg wrote to Henriette Roland-Holst after the publication of the latter's book on the general strike, which followed Kautsky's ideas and was firmly based on the attitude of the International Congress held at Amsterdam, 'what I found unacceptable in your otherwise excellent book is that you in fact treated the general strike far too formalistically as a means of defence and in that connection laid far too great an emphasis on discipline and organization and did not sufficiently bring out the point that the milieu out of which the elementary phenomenon of the general strike proceeds is the historical process of the exacerbation of class contradictions.'[212] This controversy flared up again as a result of the Russian Revolution which showed the value of the general strike as a militant weapon in periods of acute tension. From this point of view it may well be said that it was greeted as a

highly important discovery after the traditional idea of revolution on the barricades had been abandoned towards the end of
last century without either the ballot box or trade union organization being able to demonstrate that they were, in fact, capable
of providing the revolutionary battle with a new weapon dialectically linked with the day-to-day struggle. Just as Marx had
greeted the Paris Commune as having finally discovered the form
of dictatorship of the proletariat which he had been talking about
for more than twenty years without succeeding in defining its
exact content, Rosa Luxemburg and her radical friends similarly
studied the lessons of history to 'discover' new methods of combat
suited to the new phase of revolutionary action.

Finally the Russian Revolution seemed to open up a new era of
class struggle and revolutionary militancy in other countries as
well. We have already mentioned Rosa Luxemburg's view that in
its attempt to create an immense world market for capitalism and
in the course of the conflicts sparked off by their attempt,
imperialism found itself unexpectedly involved in a world war;
and that the masses must be schooled to intensify their struggles
so that they should fulfil their historical role. Hitherto the
revisionists had practically succeeded in imposing their tactics
on the masses and slowly lulling them to sleep by integrating
them into the system. The major labour agitations of these
years and their intensification in 1905 under the influence of
the Russian Revolution as well as the struggles that had occurred
throughout almost the whole of Germany in connection with
the right to vote might herald a new turning point. Just as the
advance of Japanese and Russian imperialism, which had
brought about the first world war to be fought outside Europe,
was leading to even greater world conflict, so the response of the
Russian masses to war could prepare the way for the response of
the masses the world over if social democracy proved equal to
its historical task. German imperialist policies were also creating
highly tense situations in Germany and the German labour movement had to draw the appropriate lessons from the Russian experience, spur the proletariat on to intensify the struggle, foster
the alliance with the unorganized masses, not hesitate before
the prospect of a general strike if the occasion offered and not
sacrifice the basic *raison d'être* of the organization itself to the
integrity of the organization.

The debates within the German Social Democratic Party which
since the time of the Bernstein controversy had been mainly concerned with matters of doctrine now shifted to concrete themes

of militant strategy and this time the attack on the traditional attitudes came from the left.[213] However, as Shorske remarks, this provided the opportunity for the right to show its real strength. Trade union officialdom felt itself threatened by this activism and independent spirit of the masses and for the first time went over to the counter-attack. The Trade Union Congress in Cologne which preceded the party conference was a congress devoted to the battle against the advocates of the general strike. After a long report by Bömelburg directed entirely against 'romantic revolutionaries' in contrast to the soundness and serious-ness of the establishment, a resolution was passed by 200 votes to 7 clearly rejecting the use of the general strike as part of the trade union struggle, forbidding any propaganda on its behalf, appealing to the organized workers to oppose it vigorously and urging all workers not to allow such ideas to stand in the way of their day-to-day routine activity of strengthening the trade union organization.

Quite another tone prevailed at the party conference at Jena from 17 to 21 September 1905, which had been awaited with great excitement and where the left put up a valiant fight, Rosa Luxemburg's speech was a particularly powerful one containing some of the themes of her later book: 'Every day you read reports of revolution in the newspapers . . . but it seems that you have eyes and you see not and ears and you do not hear . . . The time has come, as our great leaders Marx and Engels have predicted, when evolution turns into revolution. We can see the Russian Revolution and we should be silly fools not to learn from it.' To Heine's expression of concern that the general strike would set not only the organized but the unorganized masses on the move and to his question whether the party could curb these masses, Rosa Luxemburg replied that in revolutionary situations it was not the masses but the parliamentary lawyers that had to be curbed 'so that they don't betray the revolution'. And to those people who were scared of endangering the organization she retorted that the revolutionary spirit of enlightenment and not the organization should be given preference over all else. She re-minded the delegates that the Russian masses had been driven into revolution with 'hardly any trace of trade union organization and they are now consolidating their organization step by step by means of the struggle. It is in fact a purely mechanical and undialectical idea to think that the struggle must always be pre-ceded by strong organizations. Organization can, on the contrary, also be born as a result of the struggle, together with class consciousness.'[214]

Even Bebel found himself forced to enter the lists against the right wing and the trade unionists and succeeded in having a resolution passed by 287 votes to 14 stating that

> specifically in the case of an attack on the principle of direct, equal, secret and universal suffrage or the right to form associations, the duty of the whole working class is to resort vigorously to any means of defence that may seem appropriate. One of the most effective means of miliant action to prevent such a political crime against the working classes is, in view of the party conference, to resort in such cases to the widest possible use of a withdrawal of labour.[215]

Public opinion condemned the congress as a victory for the left and Lenin approved the resolution. Rosa Luxemburg was more cautious in her above-mentioned letter to Henriette Roland-Horst in which she justified the left wingers' support for Bebel on tactical grounds, although the latter 'has a very one-sided and superficial view of the question of a general strike'.[216]

> In fact, the Jena discussions were one of the factors which led the awareness of the German working classes to grow at the speed of the Russian Revolution, albeit on a far more limited scale. The extent of this can be judged by an unprecedented event unique in the history of the German Social Democratic Party. At the end of October 1905, the central committee of the party purged the editorial staff of *Vorwärts*. They dismissed six editors, starting with Kurt Eisner, because of their reformist policy and replaced them by radicals. Rosa Luxemburg, A. Stadthagen, Heinrich Cunow, Wilhelm Duwell and others.[217]

Yet despite this more or less obvious success, Rosa Luxemburg did not manage to impose her view that while the general strike was a thoroughly valuable and important instrument it was not to be manipulated at will or to order at a particular time according to the whim of the leaders but only when strong social tension had raised the temperature of the masses to fever pitch.

> Whether large popular demonstrations and mass action are really to take place, in whatever form, is decided by the whole complex of economic, political and psychological factors such as the state of class antagonisms at the time, the degree of enlightenment, whether the masses are ripe for militant action and these factors are imponderables that no party can create

artifically. This is the difference between major historical crises
and the minor manoeuvres that a well-disciplined party can
carry out neatly in peaceful times by wielding the big stick.[218]

Rosa Luxemburg thus opposed with equal vigour

> those who would like to order a general strike straight away by
> decision of the central committee on a fixed date in the
> calendar as well as those who would like to abolish the prob-
> lem of the general strike altogether by forbidding all propa-
> ganda for it. Both these trends consider the general strike
> merely as a technical method, a weapon, a sort of pocket-knife
> that you can keep closed in your pocket ready for any
> eventuality but that you can also decide to open and use.[219]

The Russian Revolution had taught precisely that the general
strike cannot be decided on arbitrarily, 'but that it is an
historical phenomenon, that at a given moment it arises out of
social conditions with the force of historical necessity.'[220]

But if it is true that the general strike supposes the existence
of objective and subjective conditions which make it possible
or indeed necessary, it is also true, in Rosa Luxemburg's view,
that it reacts to those conditions and creates new conditions
favourable to militant action by bringing situations to a head,
clarifying conditions, exposing the reality of society and con-
juring up new forces, new energy, a new will. So it is thus in
itself a revolutionary factor and has the rich creative revolutionary power on which Rosa Luxemburg relied as a driving force to
speed up the rate of history. Marx had already plainly drawn
attention to this when he had referred to revolt as the 'locomotive
of history'. 'To be sure all this will probably be quite different
after the revolution and the return to "normal conditions",' she
wrote from the scene of the revolution itself, 'but these events
will not pass on without leaving some trace. Meanwhile, the
achievements of the revolutions are immense: class antagonism
has been deepened, social relationships exacerbated and clarified.
And none of this is seen abroad! People imagine that the struggle
is over because it has gone underground. And at the same time
the *organization* goes indefatigably on. Despite the state of war,
the Social Democrats are energetically setting up proper trade
unions with printed membership cards, stamps, constitutions,
regular meetings, etc.'[221] Quite apart from the success or failure
of the struggle, the ups and downs of the revolutionary process,
'the most valuable thing in all this ebb and flow is the spiritual
residue left over which will be permanent: the intellectual and

cultural growth, in fits and starts, of the proletariat which is a
firm guarantee that the future progress of its economic and
political struggle is irresistible.'[222]

In view of this creative force inherent in revolution itself, it
cannot be claimed that it will only break out when all the conditions necessary for success exist together and have been closely
verified by the leaders, because some of these conditions will in
fact be realized only in the course of the struggle.

> The pedantic view of great mass movements developing in
> accordance with pre-established patterns and fixed formulas
> leads to the belief that for anyone even to be able to think of a
> general strike in Germany, it is first of all necessary for the
> railway workers to win the right of association. The natural
> and actual course of events may be exactly the opposite: that
> only a vigorous and spontaneous general strike will in fact
> obtain the right of association for the German railwaymen and
> postal workers. And the task that is insoluble under existing
> conditions in Germany will suddenly seem possible and find a
> solution through the effect and the pressure of a general mass
> political action by the proletariat.[223]

This strategy was obviously in complete contradiction to the
typical 'wait and see' attitude of the Social Democrats who explained away their revolutionary inaction by the lack of objective
conditions and the fact that neither the masses nor the situation
were ripe. To this 'wait and see' attitude Rosa Luxemburg replied
that a revolutionary crisis can ripen only in the course of the
revolutionary process and that without the active intervention
of the masses and the conscious leadership of the party towards
the ultimate goal of seizure of power, the situation can never
mature inevitably and objectively and even less so the masses
themselves; that it is only in the course of the revolutionary
struggle itself that ideology, organization and awareness can be
transformed and adapt themselves to the more advanced tasks
required of the proletariat. For this reason socialism can be
realized only by breaking through the vicious circle of stagnation,
by action arising out of the existing situation and by striving to
transcend real conflicts. This explains the statement which she so
often made during her controversy with the exponents of the
'wait and see' policy that the proletariat's seizure of power will
always be premature because maturity is achieved in the light of
experience, and because the proletariat also acquires awareness
and unity as a revolutionary class even through its failures,[224] and

this also explains why a democratic revolution can grow and develop into a socialist revolution.

Of course – and we must repeat this in order to avoid the misunderstanding into which Rosa Luxemburg's critics and interpreters have so often fallen – this creative value of revolution does not mean creating the revolution out of nothing. We have already emphasized in Rosa Luxemburg's own words, that the process cannot start unless the subjective and objective conditions exist. What she deprecates is the claim of the armchair strategists that they must have victory in their pockets before they start, who lay down the stages of the process *a priori* and fix the limits of the beginning or end of the mass action or even of the revolution itself with absolute accuracy. Just as you cannot passively wait for a revolutionary situation to turn up but have to prepare it by intervening and acting decisively, so the chapter of revolution cannot be considered as closed after an early defeat because the revolution itself creates new and more favourable conditions to launch out on to another battle. But what must definitely be avoided on the other hand is in Lenin's phrase, *Khvostism*, whereby no militant action should be taken until the whole army of the proletariat had been disciplined and organized like a proper army.

This is the supposition that the whole of the German working class to the last man and the last woman must be absorbed into the organization before we are strong enough to risk mass action which then, in accordance with the old formula, would probably turn out to be unnecessary. This is a completely Utopian theory, for the simple reason that it is self contradictory and moves in a vicious circle. Before undertaking any direct militant action the workers ought all to be organized? But the relationships and conditions of development in a bourgeois capitalist society are such that in the 'normal' course of affairs, without violent class struggles, certain sections – and in fact the greater part, the most important sections of the proletariat, those who are lowest in the social grade and most oppressed by capitalism and the State – can by their very nature not be organized. As we can see, even in England with a whole century of solid undisturbed trade union activity – apart from the Chartist movement at the beginning – without any 'romantic revolutionary' aberrations and enticements they have succeeded in organizing only a minority of the more privileged sections of the proletariat.[226]

No one with any historical sense will venture into the area of hypothesis: what would have happened if the German Social Democratic Party had accepted and applied Rosa Luxemburg's proposed revolutionary strategy? But since we are here discussing Rosa Luxemburg's doctrine of revolution theoretically we have no hesitation in concluding that it was in no way Utopian and that it probably corresponded very accurately to the opportunities of effective militant action in pre-war Germany. If these existing possibilities had all been properly exploited, if the revolutionary potential of the masses had been thrown into battle and concentrated on the objective of a struggle against the political power, as Rosa Luxemburg suggested, it is probable that Germany would have found it very difficult to risk launching into the World War and revolution would even have broken out with far greater fury before November 1918. Instead of which, as is well known, the whole weight of the Social Democratic Party was directed towards restraining the agitation, above all after 1907 when Chancellor Bülow had succeeded in weakening the Social Democrats' position by conducting his electoral campaign on the platform of nationalism and militarism. From that time onwards, the social democratic leaders' chief concern was to protect themselves from the accusation of being 'anti-national' by redoubling their patriotic fervour. In the first debate on the military estimates after the elections Noske, who was to be the 'strong man' of the anti-proletarian repression after the war, in his first important speech in the Reichstag, did not hesitate to assure the deputies that the socialists were interested in ensuring the military organization necessary for the defence of the Fatherland and that their desire for a free and highly cultivated people was to ensure that Germany should be a very strong nation.

Thus they were forced into this position either through the fear, common to all the political and trade union leaders, of compromising the organization or the fear of losing minor political positions of power, especially in Parliament, or above all through their integration, in principle, into the establishment, by now an accomplished fact. Ever since the party conference at Mannheim in 1906 the alliance of the party leadership with the trade unionists and revisionists had been dominating the party and making life increasingly difficult for the minority on the left, especially after Ebert became party secretary and chairman a few years later on Bebel's death.

In pursuit of this policy, the German Social Democrats continually strove to dissociate themselves from internationalist attitudes against imperialism and war by minimizing their dangers and as a result the party leadership finally opposed the foundation of an autonomous youth organization, proposed by Liebknecht, Zetkin, Ludwig Frank and others, because it was afraid that this would provide a focus for anti-militarist propaganda. Finally in 1913, by 52 votes to 37 with 7 abstentions, the parliamentary group supported a government proposal to establish a new tax to meet increased military expenditure. In the words of Fritz Geyer, one of the leaders of the deputies who opposed the motion, the German government now knew that they could press forward with their rearmament policy with the money which the Social Democrats had placed at their disposal through their vote. The old watchword: 'Not a mark nor a man to support the system' was no longer the central theme of the Social Democrats' parliamentary tactics; another watchword took over and was already current as early as 1907: 'In the hour of danger we shall never leave our Fatherland in the lurch.'

So it was entirely natural that, as the decisive moment of the First World War drew near, the Social Democratic leaders, although pretending to be still faithful to the old watchwords, even to the extent of calling for anti-war demonstrations, secretly reassured the Chancellor that German social democracy 'would not fail to fulfil its patriotic duty'. And the Kaiser unleashed the war in the knowledge that he could rely on the support of the strongest of the German parties. For these reasons it seems right to assume that, from this point of view, even if it cannot be asserted with complete certainty that Rosa Luxemburg's strategy would have succeeded in preventing the catastrophe of war or, at best, been able to provide a socialist solution for it, what is certain is that the attitude of the Social Democratic Party before 1914 favoured the outbreak of the First World War, just as its later attitude after the defeat effectively favoured the rise of National Socialism.

We must now examine Rosa Luxemburg's doctrine from another angle. If we believe that our previous analysis has refuted the accusation of 'revolutionary romanticism' that was continually directed against her from the right, we must now discuss the other criticism, principally directed against her by the Bolsheviks but also by others, the criticism of her 'cult of spontaneity', her underestimation of the leading role of the party, of the conscious leadership of the revolutionary struggle. As is well known, Rosa Luxemburg frequently crossed swords with Lenin over the problem of nationality, the interpretation of imperialism and the possibility of national wars in the period of imperialism and over the question of whether or not to unify the various factions into which the Russian socialist movement was split.[229] Probably their most important theoretical difference, however, concerned over the problem of party versus class and thus the role of spontaneity; the more so as this last problem was linked with the criticism of the left wing of the Social Democratic Party and especially of Rosa Luxemburg for having failed to organize the parliamentary group at the right time and then having delayed breaking away from both the Social Democratic Party and the new Independent Social Democratic Party that arose during the war, with the result that the organization of the left was unprepared to face the great events of the post-war period. Here we wish to deal with the accusations made against her 'cult of spontaneity' which, as we said, seems to us the most important of these problems.

But we cannot seriously examine this problem unless we go back to its roots. It is well known that the theoretical basis of Lenin's criticism of spontaneity is the statement which is to be found in *What is to be done?*

We have said that the workers cannot yet possess a social democratic awareness. It could only be given to them from without. The history of every country bears witness to the fact that left to themselves the working classes can only succeed in achieving a *trade union** consciousness, that is to say the conviction that it is necessary to combine into syndicates to fight the bosses, to demand such and such laws necessary for the workers, etc. Socialist doctrine arose from philosophical, historical and economic theories that had been worked out by the cultivated representatives of the property-owning classes, the intellectuals.[230]

Now Lenin's idea of the introduction of the element of consciousness into the class struggle of the proletariat from outside was taken from Kautsky and was a theory inspired by the Enlightenment and certainly not by Marx. We do not need to read many texts to convince ourselves of this, it is enough to recall the *Manifesto*,[232] the *Poverty of Philosophy*[233] or the *Draft Statutes of the International*.[234] The passages quoted in the notes show clearly enough that the proletariat can lift by itself by its own efforts to the status of a class or party, and for anyone who

* In English in the text.

knows Marx's thought, this means that it can achieve class
consciousness; until it has reached this stage, theorists are merely
Utopians and once the proletariat has finally achieved the
maturity of a party, they have only to realize what is taking
place under their eyes and spread it abroad. The theorists are thus
merely the organs of the proletariat and so far from bringing this
awareness to it from outside, on the contrary they derive their
theories from the experience of the proletariat. Whether these
theorists are bourgeois intellectuals or workers reflecting on their
own experience is purely a matter of chance and has no significance whatsoever. Even when they are of bourgeois origin, in so
far as they are the voice of the proletariat, they are integrated
into it. For Marx it is important that the working class should
become class conscious through its own struggles and, of course,
by conscious reflection on these struggles; moreover, it is sufficient
to recall Marx's commentaries on Feuerbach, particularly the
third one, to realize that Marx thought that the proletariat cannot be educated from outside (otherwise who would educate the
educators?) because, according to the theory of the inseparable
unity of theory and practice, awareness can only be reached by
practice, one's own practice and not that of anybody else, by
struggle, action and experience. Naturally the whole proletariat
does not reach the same level of awareness at one and the same
time; the most advanced and conscious part strives to lift the
other proletarians up to the level they have already achieved. The
task of this most advanced section of the most conscious militants, the Communists, as Marx said in his early works, or the
Social Democrats, as Rosa Luxemburg and Lenin called them in
their writings of this period, is to fight side by side with these
proletarians and help them to understand what they are really
fighting for, the deeper reasons of the class struggle and the
permanent interests of the proletariat as a class.

So it is in complete harmony with Marx's thought when Rosa
Luxemburg writes:

> The class struggle is obviously not the invention or the
> creation of the Social Democrats which they can switch on and
> off at will of their own accord for certain periods of time. The
> class struggle is older than social democracy; as a primary
> product of any class society, it was already alight when
> capitalism entered Europe. It is not social democracy which
> educated the modern proletariat for the class struggle but
> rather the latter that brought it into being to co-ordinate the

various local class struggles at various times and make them aware of their aims.[235]

It is plain what developments and contradictions are inherent in these different starting points. According to Kautsky and Lenin there exists an almost automatic opposition between spontaneity and awareness, with the latter being considered as coming from outside; in such cases there is the risk of permanent alienation, a clear split between the conscious element and the masses that may be a split between party and class or between the leaders and the led. The fact that in practice Lenin always succeeded in avoiding this break is due to his exceptional qualities of leadership and his constant readiness to recognize and, as far as possible, welcome the feelings and aspirations of the masses. But it is undeniable that this was a danger implicit in his theory and in the resulting mentality of the leaders; events since his death have painfully confirmed this. In Marx's view, however – and on this point he was followed by Rosa Luxemburg – the relationship between spontaneity and consciousness does not imply absolute contradiction but a dialectical transition: consciousness is born out of spontaneity and transcends it in an uninterrupted formative process which avoids any breaks in continuity, so that there is a continuous circulation between the masses and the active political elements, between class and party, between the led and the leaders not in one direction only (consciousness being communicated from those above to those below) but in both directions because consciousness itself derives from and is fed on the experience of spontaneous militant action.

However, when we talk of an 'uninterrupted formative process' of consciousness we do not mean to say that it should pour forth almost automatically like a natural product, like a glandular secretion in accordance with some 'organic' notion of the process itself. In fact, the transition from spontaneity to consciousness always involves a qualitative change, a dialectical transcendence, a transcending of one's own mistakes through self-criticism, as Rosa Luxemburg strongly insisted, a transcending of the element of immediacy by the element of reflection. We need only recall Rosa Luxemburg's opinion of the contradictory nature of the labour movement, which comprises both the factor of the day-to-day struggle for improvements within the framework of present society and the factor of the ultimate goal, that is to say the revolutionary transcendence of society itself, to see, in a sense, the same internal tension and the same dialectic in the relationship between class and party and Rosa Luxemburg was certainly right in criticizing Lenin's unfortunate remark when he said that a 'revolutionary Social Democrat' would be nothing but a Jacobin tied to the organization of class conscious workers.

> In fact [she continued] social democracy is not *tied* to the organization of the working classes (this would still indicate a certain element of alienation. L.B.) but is the specific working class movement (and as such an internal one, as we explained above. L.B.). Social democratic centralism must thus be essentially different in quality from Blanqui's. It can only be an imperative force unifying the will of the conscious, militant vanguard of the workers *vis-à-vis* their separate groups and individuals and this is, as it were, the 'self-centralism' of the leading section of the proletariat, their majority rule within their own party organization.[237]

Now in Rosa Luxemburg the two factors in this dialectical process, consciousness and spontaneity, the mass and the party, are always present and are seen in their right relationship. 'Social democracy is the most enlightened and class conscious vanguard of the proletariat. It cannot and must not stand by with folded arms waiting fatalistically for the "revolutionary situation" to turn up, that is to say, waiting for a spontaneous movement of the people to fall from heaven. On the contrary, it must, as always, hasten to anticipate the development of things and strive to speed it up;'[238] – a passage which we have already quoted in another connection. In the same article (amongst the tasks in which social democracy must give the lead in times of mass struggle) Rosa Luxemburg mentions that

> it must give the watchword for the struggle, show which path it must follow and control the tactics of the political struggle so that at every stage and at every moment of the struggle the sum total of the whole available active strength of the proletariat already committed should be fully realized and expressed in the militant attitude of the party and also that the decisiveness and vigour of the Social Democratic Party's tactics should never fall below the level of the actual relationship of forces but should rather be ahead of it: this is the most important task of 'leadership' in a period of general strike.[239]

So even for Rosa Luxemburg there existed a problem of the conscious leadership of the struggle, of its general direction but since this leadership does not descend from heaven and does not come from outside but is a factor of the unified process of proletarian struggle, a factor which finds expression in social democracy, this leadership is subject to conditions. It is conditioned first of all by the historical situation because a revolutionary socialist action can never be completely invented but can only arise as part of an historical development as a 'factor of history' as she called it[240] and only by accepting the fact that it must fit into the 'laws – that is to say the trends – of the development of society – the real movement in Marx's words – can social democracy ensure that its decisions are crowned by success.'[241] It is also conditioned by the agreement of the unorganized and unconscious masses reacting to the stimulus of events: if the party is detached from the masses and starts issuing directives that the masses cannot hear and which find no echo in the hearts of the people, then the action is doomed to failure. But if the party has successfully interpreted the course of history and taken up the right attitude to continue its development, if it remains in permanent contact with the broad masses of the people, furthers and channels and, indeed, arouses its fighting potential, never allowing a break to occur between itself and the popular masses, then mass action becomes a real movement of the people and the revolution is launched on its victorious course.

But to ensure that no break takes place between the party and the masses or between the leaders and the led, the party leadership must not confine itself to issuing orders but must make every effort to explain them, to clarify their reasons and aims, to tell the masses the truth. The mass cannot lead itself because

> like *thalassa*, the eternal sea, it conceals within itself every hidden possibility: deathly calm and raging tempest, the most abject cowardice and the wildest heroism. The mass is always what it has to be through force of circumstances and is always ready to become something completely different from what it seems.[242]

The masses must be led, but led by truth: on this point, on the revolutionary function of truth and its absolute necessity in the relationship between the leaders and the masses, Rosa Luxemburg was completely uncompromising:

> 'There is nothing so damaging to the revolution as illusions and there is nothing that serves it better than plain blunt truth.'[243]

For this reason

> if the widest possible sections of the proletariat are to be won
> over to political action undertaken by social democracy and
> if, in turn, social democracy is to seize and hold the real
> leadership in a mass movement to become the master of the
> whole movement in the political sense of the word, then it
> must make known to the proletariat as clearly, coherently and
> decisively as possible, the tactics and aims appropriate for the
> period of coming struggle.[244]

Only in this way can awareness really be formed and developed,
can the masses be encouraged to develop initiative and to learn
how to educate themselves; and only thus can even mistakes
become fruitful.

> The modern proletariat comes through these trials in a very
> different way [from the reactionary petty bourgeois]. Its errors
> are as enormous as its tasks. There is no pre-established pattern
> valid once and for all time, there is no infallible guide to show
> it the path which it must follow. Its only teacher is the
> experience of history, the thorny path of its self-emancipation
> is paved not only with infinite suffering but also with innumer-
> able errors. The goal of its journey, its emancipation, depends
> on the question as to whether the proletariat is capable of
> learning from its own mistakes. Self-criticism, pitilessly cruel
> self-criticism, capable of penetrating to the bottom of things,
> is the light of life for the proletarian movement, the very air it
> breathes. The surrender of the socialist proletariat in the
> present world war is unprecedented in history, it is a misfor-
> tune for the whole of mankind. But socialism would be lost only
> if the international proletariat were unable to measure the
> depths of this fall and failed to learn anything from it all.[245]

In this context the meaning of the famous phrase with which
Rosa Luxemburg ends her controversy against Lenin's centralistic
principle in 1904 becomes clear.

> The false steps which a real revolutionary labour movement
> makes are historically immeasurably more fruitful and valu-
> able that the infallibility of the best central committee.[246]

In other words, if there is no gulf between the leaders and the
masses, if there exists between the two the constant dialectical
relationship which we indicated, if the masses thus act in accordance with their spontaneous impulse and are enabled by the party

to understand its reason and its objectives, then even if the action should lead to mistake and failure, the error would be a fruitful one. But if the masses are ordered about or only called upon to act when it suits the leaders then the dialectical relationship is lacking, a break occurs, followed by a relapse into Blanquism[247] which on this point is clearly differentiated from Marxism in the sense that it does not call upon the masses to participate constantly and consciously in the political struggle but mobilizes it only in support of the decisions of the leaders in accordance with the plans of a conspiracy which has taken place without any contact with and without the knowledge of the masses.[248] We know that after the experience of the 1905 Revolution in Russia, Rosa Luxemburg herself rejected the accusation of Blanquism which the Mensheviks made against Lenin but the difference of opinion which we have mentioned remained essentially unchanged on the questions of spontaneity, of organization and leadership from above.

Her controversy with Lenin over the question of organization was a particularly lively one and Lenin never missed the opportunity of denouncing her conception of organization as a process. Of what did this process consist? In her controversy with Lenin in 1904 Rosa Luxemburg had written that, historically,

> social democracy springs from the elementary class struggle. It is thus caught up in the dialectical contradiction that, on the one hand, the proletarian army is recruited only during the course of the struggle and on the other, that it is only in the course of the struggle that it becomes clear in its own mind as to its aims. Organization, understanding and struggle are not here independent factors, mechanically separated from each other even in time, as in Blanqui's conception of a movement, but are merely different facets of the same process. On the one hand, apart from the general principles of the struggle there are no ready-made, detailed tactics, established in advance, in which the members of the Social Democratic Party could be drilled by a central committee. On the other hand, the course of the struggle which creates the organization causes continual fluctuation in the sphere of influence of social democracy.[250]

This idea of Rosa Luxemburg's, though essentially sound, certainly contains the danger of ignoring certain necessary distinctions. Of course, class consciousness is formed in the course of the struggle, that is in the course of the historical process and the organiza-

tional structures become modified and transformed and adapted
to mobile situations; consequently, her criticism of rigid, close
and static organization, organization for the sake of organization,
is thoroughly justified but this criticism must not extend to completely denigrating the factor or organization and claiming that
from time to time forms of organization must be dispensed with
in favour of the creative spontaneity of the masses. In this sense
Lukács was right when he wrote that she had shown great
perspicuity in perceiving the limitations of the traditional conception of organization which is wrong in its relation to the
masses and that she had made a great step forward towards a
clear recognition of the problem of organization by removing it
from its abstract isolation and inserting it into the historical process but that in so doing she undoubtedly made the mistake of
thinking of the struggle of the masses as being possible without
the intermediary of the party and its organization or at least of
strongly underrating this factor. Nevertheless, it is only right to
recognize that this enabled Rosa Luxemburg to understand
the importance of the unorganized masses in the revolutionary
process and to be the first to see the value of new forms of
organization. In this connection, Zinoviev's evidence is particularly significant:

> I remember my chats with Rosa Luxemburg in Kuokalla in
> 1906, in Lenin's tiny flat where he was living more or less in
> exile. It was Rosa Luxemburg who first tackled the task of
> writing a theoretical account of the causes leading to the
> failure of the revolution; and she was the first of the militant
> Marxists to understand the mean of the Soviets even in 1905,
> when they were only in the planning stage.[251]

We can say, substantially, that on the theoretical level no strong
objections in principle can be raised to Rosa Luxemburg's conception, but in practice she was occasionally inclined to overestimate
the spontaneous element, in contrast to Lenin whose statements
on this point are frequently less dogmatic but whose practical
qualities of leadership, even in the most difficult circumstances,
were quite unparalleled. So if we cannot say that Rosa Luxemburg
advanced a real 'theory of spontaneity', we can speak of her
excessive belief in the spontaneous initiative of the masses which
was frequently demonstrated in practice and, as Flechtheim
recently wrote, she was inclined to see the masses in the same
light as Eisenstein saw the Odessa crowd in the *Battleship
Potemkin*.[252] Yet this attitude is to a considerable extent due to

her reaction against the situation of the German labour movement, against 'the bureaucracy and a certain narrow-mindedness'
of the trade union officials who hindered the growth of the movement,[253] against the pretention to impose on the masses 'the
purely passive virtue of discipline'[254] as a duty, against the constant danger that the party officials should consider themselves as
'professionally entitled to control the initiative and leadership of
the local life of the party and treat the members as mere rubber-
stamps'[255] against the essentially conservative role 'of the social
democratic leadership'[256] and in general against the policy of
going slow, avoiding crises, and of downright surrender of the
leaders. There is no doubt that in the actual conditions of the
German Social Democratic Party, mass action represented a way
of breaking up the ossified bureaucracy and conservatism of the
party apparatus and party organization and was the only source
of new methods of struggle and of more progressive aims. But
that Rosa Luxemburg was able to understand the value of revolutionary leadership is proved by the fact that in the Polish Social
Democratic Party which had, in fact, a revolutionary leadership
to which she belonged, the role of leadership was never underestimated and that when she drew up the plans for a new revolutionary Internationale for after the war, she emphasized the
necessity of a centralized leadership, thereby incurring the
criticism of Liebknecht who in fact defended the spontaneity of
the masses against Rosa Luxemburg herself.[257]

Another of Rosa Luxemburg's attitudes which had been criticized in connection with her underestimation of the question of
organization is, as we have already indicated, the failure to form
a left wing section inside the Social Democratic Party and the
delay in forming a breakaway group and thus an autonomous
party after the events of the war. It is undeniably true that the
formation of a separate group or indeed of an autonomous party
becomes a necessity for genuinely militant socialists when the
policy of the ruling majority is a policy of surrender and thus of
integration into capitalist society, but it must also be pointed out
that such an attitude conflicted with the nature of social democracy at that time. Indeed there is little point in making any
comparison with Lenin who was militating in a newly-formed
party, whose main leaders were living in exile and had no large
masses to organize, whereas when Rosa Luxemburg joined the
German Social Democratic Party in 1898, it had been in existence
for thirty-five years, was strongly organized and had always
prized the unity of the working classes as a great achievement

and indeed was considered by all as 'the' party of the working classes. Any attempt to split it would have met with resounding failure, not only because of the built-in durability of all workers' organizations but above all because of the particular strength of German social democracy, both at the organizational and the psychological level. Even the formation of a splinter group was difficult for similar reasons and also because for many years it was the left wing of the Social Democratic Party itself which had been fanatical supporters of discipline against the right wing which in practice violated the decisions of congress.

Nevertheless, from early in 1913, a start was made in the organization of a splinter group with the creation of a cyclo-styled review called *Sozialistische Korrespondenz* by Rosa Luxemburg, Mehring and Karski-Marchlewski; but the cohesive force of the party and the fear of undisciplined acts were such that even after 4 August 1914, that is to say after the *volte-face* of the leadership in trampling under foot the most solemn decisions of congress and its most deeply rooted traditions, it was not possible for Rosa Luxemburg to find more than two other signatories for a proposed protest;[258] and Karl Liebknecht was not one of them not, of course, because he lacked the courage but because he felt that any lack of discipline at that time would in fact have isolated him from the masses on whom he was relying for future action and whom he could only approach as a comrade and party member.[259] If other authoritative and seriously committed comrades rejected the thought of showing lack of discipline for the same reason, even more were they logically bound to reject the idea of a splinter group. 'In our actions, we did not for one instant think of splitting the party', as one of those prominently involved in this incident recently wrote.[260] No doubt the reluctance of Rosa Luxemburg and her comrades to launch out on the path of splitting the party and the Internationale sprang from their general political attitude: the stronger the move to shift the centre of gravity from the top to the bottom, from the leaders to the class, the stronger the feeling of the need for unity and homogeneity and so, if a split became necessary, the centre of gravity would be shifted all the more strongly upwards towards the leadership. So historical reasons and reasons of principle combined to delay the split. But it cannot be said that at a given moment Rosa Luxemburg failed to recognize its necessity and did not direct her efforts in that direction,[261] although she was always aware of the necessity of maintaining contact with the masses and ensuring that the split should be as violent as possible even in the lower levels of the party. Thus it would be difficult to pass a pure judgement of principle on this question: we cannot talk of splinter groups or split in the abstract because when we are dealing with living political action, there are too many factors involved in any judgement on the concrete expediency of acting in a particular way and, above all, in acting at a particular moment in a particular way. Our conclusion on this point would be that Lenin was right to say that the masses cannot themselves spontaneously direct the struggle for socialism which presupposes a highly developed degree of awareness. Rosa Luxemburg would not disagree and indeed recognized the necessity of such leadership but in practice underestimated its role and was certainly wrong in so doing; but in our view she was correct in her view that this leadership factor is not the sole prerogative of the leaders, external to and above the masses, existing without their spontaneous participation and the direct experience of the development of class consciousness which is the real strength of the socialist movement. Far from being opposed, therefore, the two factors of leadership and spontaneity represent the end product of a synthesis in the sense that without the experience of the masses, able leaders cannot be formed either and this in turn is an important factor of success, always provided that the ability of the leaders is continuously integrated into the consciousness of the masses.

We must now consider Rosa Luxemburg's concrete reactions to the Russian and German Revolutions during the years from 1917 to 1919.

We have already seen the importance she attached to the Russian Revolution and mentioned at least four things which justified her interest:

(a) as early as the end of the nineteenth century she had recognized the revolutionary nature of the Russian Revolution and realized that world revolution might be sparked off there;

(b) during the 1905 Revolution she had emphasized its socialist character inasmuch as the level of development of the Russian economy and society had not enabled the bourgeoisie to have either the strength or the political will to undertake the leadership of a revolution and only the socialist proletariat could undertake this role.

(c) also during the 1905 Revolution she had recognized the revolutionary value of the new weapon forged by the proletariat, the soviets, which in contrast to mere parliamentary participation had the advantage of not constricting revolutionary class feeling into an organization that had grown out of the old system.

(d) finally she had always pointed out how valuable the Russian Revolution was from the international point of view and its direct interest for the European and above all for the German proletariat which must find fresh impetus for its own revolutionary struggle in the Revolution in Russia.

Thus it was plain that she would follow the events of the first phase of the Russian Revolution (March 1917) with passionate interest and predict its most important developments. In a letter dated April 1917, she wrote to Marta Rosenbaum that the events in Russia were having the effect of an 'elixir of life' and that they were a 'promise of salvation, for all of us', though she added, 'I'm afraid that none of you appreciates it properly, because you don't realize sufficiently well that it is our cause that is winning over there.' And although the Revolution had only just begun and Prince Lwow's provisional government had been established, she predicted that the effects of the Revolution would be felt throughout the whole world and would extend to the whole of Europe:

> I am firmly convinced that a new era is beginning.[262] And at the same stage she wrote to the same friend: 'And so Kautsky can't find anything better to say than that social conditions in Russia are not yet ripe for the dictatorship of the proletariat! Fortunately history is far from following Kautsky's theoretical rules, so let's hope for the best.'[263]

This opposition between Kautsky's and Rosa Luxemburg's views was expressed at the same time in the papers of the two groups whose theories they represented: there were the independent socialists who had formed themselves as a party independent of the Social Democratic Party at the Party Conference at Gotha (6–8 April 1917) and the Spartakus Group which although belonging to the same party pursued its own policy and ideology. Whereas the independents considered the March Revolution merely as a possible contribution to peace without having any inkling of its socialist development,[264] as early as April 1917 Rosa Luxemburg was writing that 'victory over the Tsarist regime was not the end but only a mild beginning' and added that the retreat of the bourgeoisie from its temporarily progressive position of determined liberalism would follow logically and inevitably in the

near or distant future as a result of its generally reactionary
nature and its class opposition to the proletariat. And in the same
article we read:

> Any peace movement in Russia or elsewhere can only take
> one form, a revolutionary class struggle against its own bour-
> geoisie, a struggle for political power in the State. These are
> the inescapable future prospects of Russian revolutions. Far
> from having ended its work it has only provided a bare intro-
> duction to it which will be followed by the most violent
> struggles for peace and for the radical programme of the
> proletariat.[265]

Even after the Bolsheviks' failure in July, Rosa Luxemburg believed in the further development of the Russian Revolution
towards socialism. In August she wrote in *Spartakus* that

> in the long or short run the new coalition government will
> have to give way, through the internal logic of its develop-
> ment, that is to say to an actual formal dictatorship of the
> proletariat.[266]

For this reason she was greatly delighted by the October
Revolution, that long desired event out of which international
revolution would develop.

> *In politics* you must certainly be like me. I rush to read every
> new paper for news from Petersburg but one still can't see
> what is happening. Unfortunately, it is most unlikely that
> Lenin and his friends will be able to stay in power in this
> frightful state of chaos and indifference in the west. But even
> the attempt is epoch-making.[267]

The indifference of the Western European masses was a sore
point for Rosa Luxemburg, as the proof of the failure of the whole
socialist movement in the west which had lost all sense of internationalism and at the same time all revolutionary impetus. She
concentrated all her arguments and those of the Spartakus movement as a whole on this point, against the new Independent
Socialist Party to which they formally belonged. As early as
April 1971 Rosa Luxemburg pointed out, in opposition to the
Independents (who considered a revolution impossible in Germany because it would have to take place against the organized
might of the military state) that workers and military soviets

could become an instrument in the service of the people and the
revolution 'if − if only the proletariat is revolutionary.'[268] This
lack of revolutionary awareness in the German proletariat that
once played a decisive historical role was the result of the policy
and education of the Social Democrats who were steeped to the
marrow in 'moronic officialdom.'[269]

But her justifiable enthusiasm for the October Revolution never
led her to lose her independence of judgement,[270] particularly
since the possibility of extending the Revolution to the German
proletariat depended on the ability to interpret an historically
different situation if one were not to propose a mechanical
repetition of the Russian experience. For this reason, not only
must the Revolution's unavoidable errors be promptly recognized
but also the essential compromises arising from the necessity to
adapt to circumstances which must nevertheless not be taken as a
model for different sorts of situation. Only by keeping this in mind
can we understand what Rosa Luxemburg wrote on this subject:[271] in her prison cell in Breslau she was not in a position to
put forward the practical solutions that the Bolsheviks ought to
have found but she did strive to ensure that these practical solutions, fully justified in their Russian context, were not made into a
universal dogma. It was true that her isolation in prison
strengthened her personal need to clarify the circumstances of the
class struggle and this endeavour did lead her to excessive simpli-
fication and thus to distortions of the truth. In this sense, Lukács'
criticism of Rosa Luxemburg's work on the Russian Revolution is
justified when he reproaches her for overestimating its purely
proletarian nature, that is overestimating both the external
strength and the inner understanding and maturity which the
proletarian class can possess and did actually possess in the first
stage of the Revolution and, equally, underestimating the non-
proletarian elements outside the proletarian class as well as the
strength of these ideologies within the proletariat itself.[272]

Her essay on the Russian Revolution contains several criticisms
of the work of the Bolsheviks. The three most important were:

1. Their belief in a people's right to self-determination and
their repeated recognition of the right of every people to enjoy
this right even if it meant partitioning a state.
2. The distribution of land to the peasants.
3. The problem of dictatorship and democracy.

The first of these criticisms took up an argument that was at the
heart of Rosa Luxemburg's thinking as a leading member of the

Polish labour movement and with which we have not yet been able to concern ourselves. Let us therefore briefly consider the historical antecedents of the question.

Rosa Luxemburg's attitude towards the question of nationality with regard to Poland, which at that time was partitioned into three parts under Russia, Germany and Austria, was a subject of constant and relentless dispute with Poland's Socialist Party (the PPS) and later on with Lenin and the Bolsheviks. For the PPS the re-unification and re-establishment of an independent Polish state was a matter of first priority, even for the proletariat, whereas Rosa Luxemburg and her colleagues considered this idea misguided and liable to attract the proletariat away from its class responsibilities. In order to persuade the Polish proletariat to follow the Marxist line – meaning by this the line of the class struggle and internationalism – and in order to resist the nationalistic and petty bourgeois deviationism of the PPS, a group of Polish exiles, Rosa Luxemburg, Leo Tyszka (Jogiches), Adolphus Warszawski (Warski) and Julian Marchlevski (Karski) founded a review called *Sprawa Robotnicza* (The Cause of the Worker) which immediately became the official organ of the Social Democratic Party of the Kingdom of Poland and Lithuania (SDKPIL), founded in the same year and which as a socialist party challenged the PPS for the leadership of the Polish labour movement. Rosa Luxemburg although barely twenty years old at the time, immediately assumed the leading role in the review and in the party as their ideological leader and on behalf of the editors made a report to the International Socialist Congress in Zürich in 1893 accusing the PPS, in their desire for independence, of turning the social democratic programme into a mixture which had already won for itself the title of 'social patriotism', an expression which Lenin took up later and which finally became current coin in the course of the First World War.

Rosa Luxemburg's argument was based on the analysis of the economic and social development of Poland to which she was devoting intensive study at that time and which was the subject of her thesis for the University of Zürich.[274] According to this argument, the basis of which we cannot discuss here, until 1860 Poland was, like Russia, an agrarian country, closed and semi-feudal, without any economic connections with Russia to compensate for the occupation; this also led to the growth of her strong national feeling and the separatist movements flourished. Yet the development of capitalism later created an organic link between the two countries by providing a common market for

Russian as well as for Polish industry; indeed, the vast extent of the Russian Empire and its conquests supported the protectionist policies of Polish industry and thereby weakened the social basis of the separatist trends. According to Rosa Luxemburg, separatism remained the stamping ground for the petty bourgeois intelligentsia and the precapitalist sectors of society who found the ideology of nationalism a useful tool against the threat of capitalist expansion, but the proletariat could not join in with them because it was bound to give priority to the fight for democracy and socialism in close conjunction with the Russian proletariat. Historically, the independence of Poland seemed for Rosa Luxemburg an outdated ideal, which could, moreover, only be realized by means of a war, whereas the fight against the aristocratic regime of the Tsar and a socialist democratic revolution in the Russian empire offered an immediate goal; this argument was confirmed by events. For Rosa Luxemburg it was serving the class enemy to divert the energies of the Polish proletariat away from this revolution for the sake of a petit bourgeois ideal; hence her unrelenting and uncompromising attitude in the controversy.

This does not mean, of course, that Rosa Luxemburg and her associates ignored the distinctive national qualities of Poland; but they thought that an autonomous status within the framework of a multi-national State would satisfy the legitimate national aspirations of the Poles and at the same time would make it possible for them to take part in the impending Russian Revolution.

As a result of this controversy, Rosa Luxemburg also came into conflict with what had hitherto been the traditional position of the labour movement, which went back to the well-known views expressed by Marx and Engels on the subject. Had not the First Internationale come into being as the result of a meeting in support of Polish independence? Her reply to this argument that was so often made against her was the perfectly correct one that a true Marxist interpretation does not consist of a mere repetition of Marx's words but of a concrete historical understanding of other situations in the light of Marx's method. She interpreted Marx's 'attitude' towards Polish independence historically by showing that it was dependent on circumstances, for both Marx and Engels. Polish independence was a weapon against the Tsarist regime, the bulwark of European reaction,[276] yet even they thought that the rise of socialism would make nationalism irrelevant.[277] We shall see whether she proved right in her view that in the existing circumstances the problem of nationalism had in fact lost a great deal of its relevance and was a factor likely to delay the socialist revolution.

That the danger of the PPS's social patriotic attitude was, as Rosa Luxemburg feared, a real one was proved by the behaviour of many of its leaders during the 1905 Revolution; they tried hard to separate the action of the Polish proletariat from that of the Russian proletariat and were far more concerned to unite all classes in Poland in support of independence. They carried this policy to the point of preventing strikes and militant action by the Polish workers against Polish industrialists.[278] After independence was achieved the Polish Socialist right wing ended up as nationalist and its leader Pilsudski became Poland's Fascist dictator.

Nettl[279] rightly remarks that in the heat of her argument, Rosa Luxemburg was often inclined to lump together the attitudes of the left wing of the PPS and ultimately of the Russian Bolsheviks with the nationalistic attitudes of the Socialist right wing; the Bolsheviks indeed rejected nationalism but felt that the labour movement would be losing touch with reality if it did not stand up for the independence of Poland. In fact, Rosa Luxemburg's party never succeeded in impressing its views on the petit bourgeoisie and the peasants.

It would be difficult to settle the question of the conflict between Lenin and Rosa Luxemburg as a question of principle, as if one or other of their views was the progressive one. Lenin adopted the principle, which had been developed by Kautsky, that under capitalism the national State is the normal rule and the State made up of various nations is something either abnormal or underdeveloped;[280] whereas Rosa Luxemburg would never agree that every State must go through every stage that had been gone through in the course of history and perhaps rather precipitately imagined that an imperialistic stage of development had been reached which would create supernational, organically linked economies, possessing their bourgeoisies capable of competing with the solidarity of the working classes.

The two disputants certainly allowed themselves to be occasionally led astray into expressing excessively dogmatic views but these views must obviously be examined in the general political and social context of the time and judged with due regard to the overall strategy of the labour movement.

They were in fact in agreement on the question of method. Lenin wrote:

One absolute essential of Marxist theory when examining any social question of whatever sort is to set it in a *specific* historical context and furthermore when you are dealing with one country (as, for example, the nationalist programme for a particular country) to take into account the concrete peculiarities which distinguish that country from other countries in one and the same historical period . . . We are dealing with the nationalist programme of the Marxists of a particular country, Russia, and of a particular period, the beginning of the twentieth century. Perhaps Rosa Luxemburg is asking the question, what historical period is Russia passing through, what are the concrete peculiarities of the national programme and the national movements of this particular country at this particular time? Yet Rosa Luxemburg herself has not breathed a word about all this. She shows no sign of any analysis of the question of nationality in *Russia* in this particular period of time and the special peculiarities of Russia in this regard! [281]

Rosa Luxemburg starts from the same considerations of method as Lenin. She wrote:

In Poland it was not a question of discovering the pattern of capitalist phenomena typical for every country but of elucidating the specific social phenomena of Poland as created by capitalism and having regard to the country's special historical and political conditions. In short, it was not a question of applying the general results of Marxist analysis to the bourgeois Poland and at the same time of bringing socialism firmly down to earth from nebulous abstraction and empty pattern-building to the concrete reality of Poland. [282]

As a result of this concrete analysis she did not indeed draw any general conclusions against the right of self-determination, the validity of which she never disputed but merely its effectiveness in the situation of Poland at the time. [283] She did, however, draw special conclusions for the Polish labour movement.

For us Polish socialists the most important question today, in order to be able to adopt an attitude towards every social phenomenon, is how this attitude will effect the class interests of the Polish proletariat. The objective analysis of the social evolution of Poland leads to the conclusion that the trends towards a re-establishment of a Polish State *at this time* are a petit bourgeois Utopia; as such, they are suited only to confuse the proletariat's class struggle and lead it astray. [284]

These two texts may provide the key to enable us to fit Lenin's and Rosa Luxemburg's attitudes into their correct historical context. Lenin starts from the conditions existing in Russia, Rosa Luxemburg from those existing in Poland. Since Lenin was thinking as a Russian revolutionary, he considered all the enemies of the Tsar as allies; even the nationalism of oppressed countries, although bearing a petit bourgeois stamp, is a weapon against the Tsarist regime.[285] As a Polish revolutionary on the other hand, Rosa Luxemburg is primarily concerned to make the Polish proletariat class-conscious and to set it on the right political course, thereby placing it in the forefront of the historical process and preventing it from bringing up the rear under petit bourgeois influence, not in order to provide it with any motive to break away from the Russian proletariat but to strengthen the alliance and prevent the proletariat from expending its strength in a struggle led by the forces of the bourgeoisie. In another essay on this theme, far more moderate in tone than the previous one, Lenin came to quite similar conclusions. After remarking that 'the Dutch and Polish Marxists who oppose the right of self-determination' are doubtless 'amongst the best revolutionary and internationalist members of the international social democratic movement', he asked himself where the root of their 'mistakes' might be and replied that their attitude is to be explained

by the special objective conditions in their countries. . . . But we need only peel off this obviously faulty outer covering of their general arguments and look at the heart of the matter from the point of view of the uniquely special conditions of Holland and Poland to understand that their peculiar attitude is completely justified. . . . All this is correct with regard to the watchword of Polish independence *here and now*, because even a revolution in Poland alone would not bring any change here, the attention of the Polish masses would merely be diverted from the main cause, the connection between their struggle and the struggle of the Russian and German proletariats. It is not a paradox but a fact that the Polish proletariat as such can today serve the cause of socialism and freedom, even that of the Poles, only if it fights *shoulder to shoulder* with the proletariats of the neighbouring countries against *narrow* Polish nationalists. It is impossible to deny the great historical merit of the Polish Social Democrats in their struggle against the latter. But those same arguments which are correct in the context of the special conditions in Poland at the present time are obviously false in the generalized form in which they have been put forward. The situation is no doubt very confused but there is one way out for *all* the internationalists involved to follow: for the Russian and German Social Democrats to demand Poland's unconditional 'right to secede' and for the Polish Social Democrats to fight for the unity of the proletarian struggle in a small as well as in larger countries but without applying the watchword of Polish independence to the particular period of time.[286]

We have quoted so extensively from this text of Lenin's, frequently ignored by critics of Rosa Luxemburg, in order to show the mistake that is often made by people looking for complete and blunt contradiction between the two leaders of the Marxist left. In the middle of the war which was intended to realize Poland's claim for unity and independence and did in fact do so, on the eve moreover of the outbreak of a new revolution in Russia (his article was written in October 1916), Lenin acknowledged the great merit of Rosa Luxemburg and her colleagues in their struggle against Polish nationalism and admitted that the correct attitude for the Polish Social Democrats was not to raise the claim for Polish independence at the present time. But had not Rosa Luxemburg in fact said that the watchword of Polish independence was not relevant for the Polish proletariat 'at the present moment'?[287]

We thus feel justified in concluding that Rosa Luxemburg had quite clearly seen the danger for the labour movement of supporting the trend towards independence since it could not be realized without at least a European war which could certainly not be a socialist aim and because, in addition, in any war primarily concerned with questions of nationality, the leadership would undoubtedly fall into the hands of the petit bourgeoisie. This would relegate the working class to a subordinate role and shift any prospects of socialism into the distant future.

Yet as on other occasions in the course of her strictly logical exposition of a problem, she allowed herself to be led astray and overlook certain aspects of reality which, although doomed to disappear eventually, were at the moment both present and active, such as for example the concrete meaning of the question of nationality in the hearts of the Polish people. The result of this attitude was, in practice, the isolation of her party from the pre-capitalist sectors of the peasants and petit bourgeoisie. Rosa Luxemburg generally tended to underestimate these sectors, since she emphasized the historical trends of capitalist development, and thus precisely the need to overcome precapitalist phases, sectors and mental attitudes. To sum up, it cannot be denied that Rosa Luxemburg underestimated the strength of the national feeling of the Poles but from the revolutionary point of view it is understandable that she was interested in opposing everything which might be exploited by this feeling and prevent the creation of a class-consciousness. And it is also understandable that she feared that the Polish proletariat might, as a result of this national feeling, be cut off from the revolution at the very moment when there was reason to hope that the success of socialism in Russia might provide a solution acceptable to the Poles by creating a multinational State.

Lenin, however, with his extraordinary capacity for grasping the contingent aspects of a situation and adapting his tactics to the one offering the greatest possibilities at least cost, intuitively understood the contribution that anti-Russian nationalism could make to the struggle against the Tsarsist regime and tried to encourage it, even if he occasionally gave a somewhat dubious doctrinaire tinge to these tactical attitudes. But when it came to the point, that he also did not believe that the different nations of the former Tsarist empire had 'the right to secede' which he had himself proclaimed, was shown when he reconquered, in the name of the Revolution, the countries which had broken free, eg Georgia.

The second criticism of Rosa Luxemburg to which we referred concerns the slogan: 'land for the peasants'. Here too it is obvious that Lenin was at that time conditioned by tactical necessity and if Rosa Luxemburg was also right to be scared of the difficulties which would arise for the future establishment of socialism as a result of the fragmentation of the large estates (as events subsequently proved), yet once again she made the mistake, for which Lukács criticized her and which we mentioned above, namely that of overestimating the purely proletarian nature of the Russian Revolution and underestimating the importance of the non-proletarian elements which were so strongly represented in Russian society. However, her historical sense enabled her to rectify this mistake and she wrote to her comrade Warski from prison:

> True, the agrarian conditions that have been created are the sorest and most dangerous point in the Russian Revolution. But even here it is true that the greatest revolution can only

complete what has already developed to the right stage of maturity.[289]

Anyone now reading, thirty-five years later (of course with Marxist eyes), what she wrote on socialist democracy, cannot fail to be fascinated. She was in complete agreement with the Bolsheviks as to the tasks of the revolution:

> The Bolsheviks immediately established a completely revolutionary programme on the broadest possible lines as the aim of their seizure of power; not the consolidation of bourgeois democracy but the dictatorship of the proletariat with a view to the realization of socialism. Thereby they have won undying historical fame as the first people ever to proclaim the ultimate goals of socialism as a programme of immediate practical politics.[290]

But

> the dictatorship of the proletariat is democracy, in the socialist sense of the word. The dictatorship of the proletariat . . . is the use of every means of political power to realize socialism, to expropriate the capitalist class in accordance with the feeling and through the will of the revolutionary majority of the proletariat, that is to say in the spirit of social democracy. Without the conscious will and the conscious action of the proletariat there can be no socialism.[291]

> It is the historical mission of the proletariat when it achieves power to create socialist democracy in place of bourgeois democracy, not to destroy every form of democracy . . . Socialist democracy begins both with the destruction of class domination and the construction of socialism. It begins from the moment when the socialist party seizes power. It is nothing but the dictatorship of the proletariat.[292]

So the dictatorship of the proletariat is not the negation of democracy, as Kautsky and, from the opposite point of view, Lenin and Trotsky seemed to think but the principle of socialist democracy, because it is the dictatorship of the whole class and not only of the party.

We see here once again the old conflict between Rosa Luxemburg and Lenin and once more we have to say that Rosa Luxemburg's account of the principles of the dictatorship of the proletariat is perfectly in accordance with Marx's teaching. But these principles were valid for a socialist revolution in the conditions which Marx had always had in mind, that is to say for a revolution occurring in a highly advanced capitalist country and not in a backward country like Russia in 1917, where the conditions for such a dictatorship of the proletariat were completely lacking, a revolution which would permit the full development of socialist democracy, the broadest and most unrestricted democracy, 'freedom for those who think differently'.[293] Rosa Luxemburg was certainly right in thinking that socialism can only come to fruition thanks to the initiative, the creative ability and the participation of the masses; that 'decrees, the dictatorial power of factory inspectors, ferocious punishment, terrorism are only palliative measures'; that the only way to achieve a rebirth was 'in the school of public life itself' but was this possible in the Russia of the day, with a proletariat that was largely unprepared, with the immense problems that needed solving, with the threat of capitalist aggression and the civil war which was then raging?[295] But above all with the weakness of the international proletariat and Russia's isolation? Rosa Luxemburg realized this herself when she wrote:

> Everything that is happening in Russia can be explained: it is an inevitable chain of cause and effect whose starting and finishing points are the failings of the German proletariat and the occupation of Russia by German imperialism. It would be asking a superhuman effort from Lenin and his colleagues to expect them to produce in such conditions, almost by magic, the best democracy, a model dictatorship of the proletariat and a flourishing socialist economy.[296]

These words are a sufficient reply to some of Rosa Luxemburg's criticisms of the Bolsheviks, for example that of having dissolved the constituent assembly. There is no doubt that had they submitted to the constituent assembly, where they were in the minority, they would never have brought about the revolution and they would not have wished that at any price. In any case, it is probable that on this point she later changed her mind, as her German colleagues maintained, because during the fiery days of November and December 1918 she spoke out resolutely against calling a German constituent assembly and in favour of giving power to the workers' and soldiers' councils.[297]

So if it is true that, in the terms in which it was expressed, Rosa Luxemburg's criticism sinned against the historical reality of the particular moment which demanded a strongly centralized power, it is also true that the spirit of this criticism is not only in accordance with the main line of Marxism but is also the spirit that should inspire every Marxist revolutionary leader. If Rosa Luxemburg had found herself shoulder to shoulder with the Bolsheviks during these years of the Russian Revolution or if she had managed to become the leader of a successful German revolution, her sense of concrete reality would assuredly have forced her to undertake a series of forcible actions and to a centralization of power that she had not foreseen immediately before. In this sense, her attitudes between November 1918 and January 1919 are extremely significant and there is no doubt that had she been fighting for the victory or defeat of the revolution against an insidious enemy lurking in every corner, she would not have hesitated to act quite ruthlessly. But she would never at any moment have failed to recognize that these were exceptional measures, nor ever have forgotten that she must at all times strive to achieve the greatest possible participation of the masses and the highest possible measure of democracy. Nor in her duty to tell the masses the truth and account for the actions undertaken by the revolution. Her exceptional government would really have been an exception and have followed a line of development that would lead to the creation of democratic conditions as soon as possible. For this reason her sharpest criticism of the Bolsheviks was probably her final one when she accused them of building their theories on a purely contingent basis and turning the exception into a rule of conduct.

In their resolutely revolutionary attitude, their exemplary energy and unshakeable loyalty to international socialism they really accomplished all that could be accomplished in such diabolically difficult circumstances. The danger arises at the moment when, making a virtue of necessity, they lay down rigidly in every detail the theory of the tactics that have been forced on them by the inevitable pressure of circumstances and recommend them as a model of socialist tactics, to be imitated by the international proletariat. Since in so doing they show themselves in a false light and hide their real and indisputable contribution to history under the bushel of deviations imposed on them by necessity, they do an ill-service to the international socialism for which they have fought and suffered by wanting to introduce into it, as new doctrines, all the distortions forced on Russia by dire necessity – distortions that were ultimately merely the reflection of the bankruptcy of international socialism during this world war ... They cannot

hope to work miracles – and an exemplary and perfect pro-
letàrian revolution accomplished in an isolated country
exhausted by the world war, throttled by imperialism, and
betrayed by international socialism would indeed be a miracle.
The important thing is to distinguish in the Bolsheviks' policies
the essential from the inessential, the substance from the
accidental.[299]

That this criticism hit the mark and pointed to a real danger is
sufficiently shown by the trend, which reached giant proportions
after Lenin's death, towards making the uniquely original experience of the Russian Revolution a 'model for socialist tactics',
to the point of turning it into a fixed, universally valid pattern,
indeed a dogma of faith. We believe also that she was right in
her judgement that it was 'an ill-service to international socialism'
to make it accept not only the immense positive contribution of
the October Revolution but also as new doctrines, all the distortions forced on Russia by dire necessity and we are firmly
convinced that Rosa Luxemburg's thought can be of great help
in trying to overcome the errors which now beset labour movements.

Her explanation of the root cause of these errors, that is to say
the international isolation of Russia, is certainly equally valid.
In agreement with Marx and Lenin she believed that a revolution
in Russia might bring the working classes to power but that 'the
fate of the Russian Revolution was completely dependent on
international events'.[300] The fact that after the failure of the
international revolution, Russia had been able to continue alone
on the path of socialism does not invalidate her argument which
in this case is no different from the attitude of Lenin; in reality the
establishment of socialism in Russia alone, which was the only
choice open to the Bolsheviks, cost infinitely more blood and tears
than would otherwise have been the case and the responsibility
for this does not only fall on Stalin but also and above all on the
international labour movement that left Russia in this state of
isolation. This is another valid conclusion of Rosa Luxemburg's
writings, where her analysis is supported by her deeply felt feeling
of internationalism.

Perhaps no one was more conscious than she of the international character of the labour movement and the close links
between the events in the struggles taking place in the various
countries.[301] At a time when the Western European labour movement was already launched on the path which it continued to

follow, that of increasing integration into capitalist society, Rosa
Luxemburg firmly supported the cause of internationalism, not
only because she belonged both to the Russo–Polish and the
German movements, not only because of the almost religious
bond she felt with the whole of mankind[302] but as a result of her
own studies. As the imperialistic policies which she analysed so
acutely in her writings created a tight network of international
relations that finally embraced the ruling classes of every State,
she realized that the anti-imperialist and anti-capitalist struggle
of the proletariat could not take place in a vacuum within each
isolated State. She was led to this conclusion by her conception of
the historical process which strove to grasp all the effects and
implications of every single moment and place them in the context of a global vision which is the only possible way for them to
be really understood.

Now as we know, up to the 1905 Revolution she had insisted
on the mutual influence of the Russian and the German labour
movements and on the need for them to combine their efforts in
order to achieve the socialist revolution. She could thus not fail
to realize that the terrible difficulties which beset the Russian
Revolution were primarily due to the German Social Democratic
Party which for years had worked to damp down the whole
revolutionary spirit of the German proletariat and used its im-
placable discipline to hold it back from the road to revolution and
from active solidarity with the Russian Revolution.[303] Rosa
Luxemburg bent all her efforts to hastening the approach of the
German revolution so as to put an end to the carnage and ensure
the triumph of socialism by means of the solidarity of the Russian
and German proletariats. As early as April 1917, that is to say
seven months before the victory of the Bolsheviks, she spoke of
the outbreak of the new Russian Revolution as 'a message of
salvation' and announced to her friend Marta Rosenbaum that, 'it
is our own cause which is winning', that 'what is coming from
Russia' will 'radiate over the whole of Europe' and that 'a new
era is now beginning'.[304] In May she wrote: 'It is the first
transitional proletarian revolution of world historical importance,
which must have repercussions on every capitalist country, and
precisely because it is a proletarian socialist struggle for power,
it can only be spread by way of revolution, in Germany or in
any other country!'[305] 'Unfortunately,' she noted in January
1918, 'the Russian Revolution, with the exception of a few
courageous efforts by the Italian proletariat, has been left in the
lurch by the proletarians of every country.'[306] And in September

1918, at the same time as she was writing her essay on the Russian Revolution published after her death, she concluded her article *Die russische Tragödie* with the words:

> There is only one solution for the tragedy in which Russia is caught up: revolt in the rear of German imperialism, a mass uprising in Germany, as a signal for the international revolutionary ending of this national massacre. Saving the honour of the Russian Revolution is at this fateful moment identical with saving the honour of the German proletariat and international socialism.[307]

A few weeks later the Revolution broke out and the war came to an end. Rosa Luxemburg who had been released from prison on 9 November, on the 18th took over the management of *Rote Fahne*, the organ of the Spartakists and launched an intensive campaign in its columns to stir up the masses.

Even today it is difficult to evaluate Rosa Luxemburg's activity in the last two months of her life from the point of view of revolutionary strategy, because despite the great prestige she enjoyed with her party colleagues, she never succeeded in imposing her line and she fell victim to the events which she had vainly tried to stem.

The starting point of her analysis was the nature of the revolution: was it purely and simply a political revolution destined to consolidate the domination of the bourgeoisie or was it also a social one destined to overthrow this class domination? Her reply was clear: the world war was the necessary consequence of the policy of imperialism and imperialism was the normal expression of capitalism when it had reached a certain stage of development; so the alternative existed between social revolution and the continuation of the policy of imperialism which, as she had already written in her Junius pamphlet, would lead to dictatorship and another world war. Only a socialist revolution could forestall these consequences and it alone would be able to guarantee a democratic and peaceful development for mankind. On the other hand, it was obvious that although, under the leadership of the Social Democratic Party, the working classes had to some extent followed the policy of imperialism, they were the only class not directly responsible for it which was at the same time having to suffer the consequences and bear the sacrifices of a war to which they were increasingly opposed. For this reason they had a right to compete for power.

So the question of the nature of the Revolution led directly to the question of power. If the Revolution were to be socialist and follow socialist aims, power must be completely taken over by the workers. On 9 and 10 November, the control of the machinery of State was smashed: The Kaiser had abdicated, the government had resigned and handed over the control of public affairs to the Social Democrats, the army was beaten and in retreat, the upper classes were scared of their responsibility and did not dare to raise their heads straightaway. On the other hand the working masses who had come down into the streets were the *de facto* lords of the land. At such a moment it would have been easy to proclaim a Socialist Republic which would, of course, have aroused the opposition of the bourgeoisie and led to civil war but which would have immediately encouraged the masses further in their struggle to consolidate their power. Yet the Social Democrats, who had compromised themselves in the imperialistic war and even owed the country an account of their behaviour, adopted a definitely hostile stand to these developments and endeavoured to exploit the victory of the people to their own advantage. The compromise which they reached with the Independent Social Democratic Party (USP) on 10 November gives the key to later developments.[309] The right wing Social Democrats, in fact, avoided denying the socialist aims of the revolution and thus avoided a collision with the deep longing of the masses and, above all, with the strongly radical Berlin proletariat led by the left wing Independent Socialists; but they wished the realization of these socialist aims to be left to some future Constituent Assembly, thus gaining time to reinforce their alliances with all the conservative forces and save the old order of things by letting the most dangerous moment of the revolutionary storm blow over. In this way they opposed the immediate proclamation of a socialist republic, although they explained that this was their party's aim, and so they were reluctant to give complete power to the workers' and soldiers' councils since that would contravene democratic principles. By accepting these compromises, the Independents brought the revolutionary impetus practically to a standstill, without being able to use the time to their own advantage.

So on 10 November a new regime was set up with a provisional government, the Council of Delegates of the People (*Rat der Volksbeauftragten*) consisting of three majority Social Democrats (Ebert, Scheidemann and Landsberg) and three Independents (Haase, Dittman and Barth), with Ebert and Haase as chairmen, and an executive body, the Executive Council (*Vollzugsrat*) elected by an assembly of representatives of the workers and soldiers and consisting of six members of each of the two parties, representatives of the workers' councils and, in addition, twelve representatives of the Berlin soldiers. The Vollzugsrat's terms of reference were not clearly defined and in practice it had little or no effective power, so that the government remained the sole real authority, and in the government, the right wing Social Democrats had marked superiority thanks to their connections with and the support of officials, the army and all the conservative forces in the country. On the other hand the Independent Socialists in the government offered no serious opposition, indeed on some basic questions, eg in the struggle against the workers' councils, the Independent Barth was on the side of the majority socialists. The duplication of power (double government), which two years before had led the soviets to overthrow the provisional government, quickly evolved in favour of the government or of the one wing of it that was in a position to manipulate the situation so as to shift any reform on to the shoulders of the future National Assembly and to create conditions such that this assembly was rendered almost entirely harmless as a revolutionary body.[310]

Nevertheless, in the weeks following 10 November the question remained open and Rosa Luxemburg's attitude was of course unequivocally in favour of power for the working classes and against the National Assembly.[311]

Yet in her ideas on the seizure of power and on the dictatorship of the proletariat, Rosa Luxemburg could never think of the former in terms of a mere putsch; she thought that the majority and, if possible, an overwhelming majority of the working classes should take over power.[312] Consequently the problem of the seizure of power by the proletariat was bound up with the necessity of giving the workers the will to make a revolution, that is to say with the necessity for the Spartakists to take over the effective leadership of the proletariat. Yet despite the great popularity enjoyed by the leader of the Spartakus League because of her courageous stand against the war, any such prospect was far from being realized. You cannot take over the leadership of a proletariat with a long tradition of organization without bringing in a broad section of the middle ranks who then really mobilize and lead the masses. But these middle ranks had remained linked to the party organization: in Berlin, to the Independent Party and its left wing represented by the *Revolutionäre Obleute* (revolutionary leaders) and in the rest of Germany, with the exception of a few towns, overwhelmingly to the old party. So the problem of taking over the leadership inside the working class became the

---

problem as to where the Spartakists should migrate: should they remain an autonomous group within the Independent Party or become an independent party themselves?

Rosa Luxemburg and Leo Jogiches were rather inclined towards the first solution: Rosa Luxemburg distrusted the revolutionary extremism unleashed by the masses and was afraid of coups and rash ventures; on the other hand she believed in the ability of the masses to be educated by participation in the struggle and wanted to be able to remain in permanent contact with them as the struggle developed. Rosa Luxemburg's opposition to splitting the party has often been criticized as having been one of the reasons for the failure of the German Revolution. The fact that there was no properly organized revolutionary party ready at the right moment was certainly a disadvantage. Nevertheless the problem is less simple than it has generally been made out to be. In fact, it was extraordinarily difficult to split the German Social Democratic Party, the only working class party, which had existed for more than half a century and possessed enormous prestige with the masses (Marx and Engels had both considered it their party and up till 1913 it had been led by the most respected party leader in Europe, August Bebel) and any split could mean breaking off all contact with the masses. For this reason, the Spartakists who had diverged from the party line ever since 1914 had in fact been waiting for the appropriate moment when a deep split appeared, under the leadership of Hugo Haase, one of the two party chairmen, and Karl Kautsky, considered the greatest Marxist theorist, who had founded the USP. Any further split in this latter party which had a majority amongst the Berlin workers (although not in the rest of Germany where the masses had generally remained loyal to Ebert's and Scheidemann's form of social democracy) ran the risk of leaving the Spartakus group in a vacuum at the very moment when they most needed the chance of speaking to the masses, leading them in their struggle and helping them to build up a revolutionary consciousness. It would have been useless to take a stand on matters of principle unless these principles could be translated into action.

The revolutionary group in Bremen had, in fact, not joined the Independent Party but had none the less been unable to form their own organization; the same thing would probably have happened to the Spartakists had they not stayed with the Independents and been able to work as their supporters until the end of the war. As long as there was a hope of bringing the Independents or at least their left wing into the revolutionary struggle, Rosa Luxemburg and Leo Jogiches considered that any breakaway would be a mistake because it would have meant putting off any possibility of revolution to a much later date, the more so as the organization of the Spartakus group was practically non-existent since its most important leaders were in gaol during the war. No comparison with the Russian situation is possible since there the split took place between leaders in exile and several years of relative peace had enabled them to go ahead with their underground organization.

The impatience of the young Spartakists and the fact that the Independents remained in the coalition government with the majority Social Democrats brought the idea of a split to a head and in December led to the foundation of a new party, the Communist Party. Yet even before this party was officially founded at the Berlin Congress which was held on 31 December and 1 January, strategic differences arose. As we know, Rosa Luxemburg was convinced that the revolutionary education of the masses could only be undertaken in the course of revolutionary struggle and that this education, intensifying as it developed, should in turn affect this struggle and attract fresh sectors of the workers: she thus rejected any revolutionary plans drawn up by a committee or as a result of a decision by party leaders and warned that it would take a long time for the revolutionary process which had now started to reach its culmination in the seizure of power.

Consequently she never tired of repeating that the time was now ripe for socialism, that the proletariat must oppose the preservation of the bourgeois order and itself take over power with the workers' and soldiers' councils in order to establish the dictatorship of the proletariat whilst at the same time pointing out that 'their activity' could 'impregnate the State with the spirit of socialism only through constant active interchange between the masses of the people and their organizations, the workers' and soldiers' councils.'[313] And she added that the struggle was no easy one, that it would last a long time and demand great sacrifices.

> The imperialistic capitalist class as the last scion of the class of exploiters outdoes all its predecessors in brutality, undisguised cynicism and baseness.

> It will fight tooth and nail to protect its holy of holies, its profit and its right to exploit, using the cold cruelty which it has shown throughout the whole history of its colonial policy and during the recent war. It will move heaven and earth

against the proletariat. It will mobilize the peasantry against the towns, incite the backward sections of the workers against those who are in the forefront of socialism, it will instigate massacres by army officers.[314]

She felt the threat of massacre hanging over her own head; she knew that apart from Liebknecht, there was no one more hated than she was by the forces of reaction and most of all by the Social Democrats in the government. In a letter of condolence to her friends, the Gecks, who had lost their son in the last few days of the war, she wrote on 18 November:

We are all the toys of blind fate and my only consolation is the grim thought that I too will perhaps soon be despatched into the other world – perhaps by a bullet fired by some member of the counter-revolution which is lurking around us.[315]

Yet not all her comrades thought as she did and the first clash occurred straightaway over the question as to whether to participate in the elections for the National Assembly. Rosa Luxemburg had been one of the first to oppose the election of a legislative assembly but when even the congress of workers' and soldiers' councils had accepted the government's proposal of a National Assembly and there was thus no further arguments against holding elections, she spoke out plainly in favour of taking part in them, since she was convinced that the electoral campaign would provide the opportunity for the new party to make its position clear to the masses and win fresh support whilst the National Assembly would then provide an admirable platform for expressing its views. This was the same attitude that Marx and Lenin had adopted in the past when opposing any refusal to vote on the part of extremists and it was a thesis that fitted perfectly into Rosa Luxemburg's long-term strategy, since she considered an electoral campaign as a stage in the progress of the masses towards revolutionary maturity.

However, the new party did not as yet possess sufficient political maturity and the majority of the congress delegates voted against the proposal of the central committee which Rosa Luxemburg and Leo Jogiches had supported; there were fifteen votes in favour of participating and sixty-two votes against. Rosa Luxemburg pointed out to the delegates that there was no comparison with the Russian situation and the dissolution of the Constituent Assembly which had been decreed by the Soviet government of Ebert and Scheidemann. But the delegates

were convinced that it was not the time for elections and
that the struggle against the National Assembly must be
continued 'through general strikes and with machine-guns'.[318]
This attitude had the gravest consequences as was to be seen
later.

A few writers have pointed out the contrast between Rosa
Luxemburg's inflammatory articles and her moderation inside the
group of leaders but this was a question of two different levels of
action which corresponded to her strategy. On the one hand, from
the outside she had constantly to try to increase the state of readiness of the masses in their struggle against the Social Democratic
government which had become the tool of all the capitalist,
militarist and reactionary forces, whereas in the group of leaders
which had, indeed, to direct the action of the masses, it was
necessary to take account of the real state of affairs, the actual
balance of forces and the need to keep any action within the
bounds of possibility.

Despite her confidence in the masses and her optimistic assessment, she knew that at that moment of time there was no possibility of a forcible confrontation with the government and she
was all the more opposed to any precipitate revolt because outside
Berlin the government was maintaining its position and there was
no basis for such a revolt. When the Social Democratic government dismissed Eichhorn, the Berlin chief of police and a member
of the Independents, and the Berlin workers reacted to the provo-
cative gesture with an impressive mass demonstration, Rosa
Luxemburg and Leo Jogiches openly denounced any idea of turning their action into violence or revolt. And though this view was
shared by the party leaders Karl Liebknecht and Wilhelm Pieck,
at a meeting with the *Obleute* and the Berlin leaders of the Independents, they accepted the proposal to move over to action and
approved the formation of a revolutionary committee under
Georg Ledebour, Karl Liebknecht and Paul Scholz. Frölich who
was present at this meeting, reported that Rosa Luxemburg had
a heated argument with Liebknecht when she learned what he had
done in acting so arbitrarily and accused him of playing fast and
loose with the party programme agreed by the congress five days
before.[317]

But now the die was cast, the masses were on the move and
'blind fate' had made its decision. Although she opposed the uprising and the provocation, which presumably *agents provocateurs*
had helped to stir up, she refused to desert her post, come what
might. 'Communists,' Marx had written, 'stand among the masses

and help them to understand what they are really fighting for,'
and Rosa Luxemburg wanted to remain amongst the masses so as
to assist the maturing process,[318] even after the social democratic
minister Noske had called imperial troops into Berlin to organize
the repression, and the assassination of the Spartakist leaders had
been publicly advocated even in the columns of *Vorwärts* and in
posters on the walls. In this connection, the historian Rosenberg
suggests that this attitude of Rosa Luxemburg's shows that she
still retained a petit bourgeois sense of decency but Zetkin's and
Lukács' theory seems to us more likely when they suggest that she
retained her faith in the unity of theory and practice right until
the end and this prevented her from deserting the masses, although
not participating in their action, but for this very reason feeling
that she must contribute to educating them.[320]

On 15 January, Rosa Luxemburg and Karl Liebknecht were
arrested by cavalry officers and murdered before they were
handed over to the prison authorities. Her body was thrown into
a canal where it was not found until some months later. 'Karl and
Rosa have fulfilled their final revolutionary duty' Leo Jogiches
wrote to Lenin as soon as he was certain of their deaths:[321] a few
weeks later Jogiches was arrested and suffered the same fate.

We ought not to conclude our examination of Rosa Luxemburg's thought without mentioning her personal qualities, her
exceptional personality which has been described as combining
'the gaiety of the happiest child, the tenderness of the tenderest
woman and the seriousness and intellectual power of the most
serious man'.[322] However, another occasion may be more appropriate to do this at greater length and here we wish only to add a
few words of final judgement on her contribution to Marxist
thought. With rare exceptions, her works have for far too long
been used purely as arguments in controversies within the labour
movement, in two typical ways. The Social Democrats used very
few of her writings, principally her *Problems of Organisation in
the Russian Social Democracy* and *The Russian Revolution*, in
order to make it appear as if she was opposed to Lenin and the
Bolsheviks, condemned the dictatorship of the proletariat and
strenuously defended democracy – bourgeois democracy, of
course. We hope to have succeeded in making it clear that Rosa
Luxemburg was the irreconcilable enemy of social democracy in
the present meaning of the word, that is to say of any socialist
policy integrated into bourgeois democracy and bourgeois society
and not directing its every action towards the destruction of
capitalist society and the seizure of power by the proletariat.[323]

The Communist Party has generally started from the assumption that Lenin was always right, that he never made a mistake and that, by definition, Rosa Luxemburg was thus wrong in all her controversies with him and that it was her merit to have gradually come closer to recognizing the rightness of his attitude. We are, however, strongly of the opinion that Lenin was above all an outstanding revolutionary leader, almost without parallel, who knew how to discover and exploit every tactical and strategic possibility in order to lead the Russian proletariat to victory. But here we can also see his limitations as a theoretician, because all too often he was forced by the circumstances of a controversy to put forward as absolute truth and model solutions, tactical decisions which were perfectly valid as such but which were extremely biased by historical conditions. Consequently anyone who reads Lenin without putting him into his historical context incurs the risk of committing gross blunders. Lenin was acting in the Russian context of his time, Rosa Luxemburg in that of Germany and Poland, and some of their differences of opinion can be explained as a result of this. Some of them we have already discussed. Here we need only point out that even Rosa Luxemburg's limitations are connected with her positive qualities. Essentially, these are two in number: on the one hand, her passionate love of humanity, her deep sense of unity with every living being, her striving towards goodness as the apogee of the human spirit, as well as her hatred of class society as created by history, gave her an almost Rousseauistic optimism and faith in human nature which sometimes affected her political judgements. On the other hand, her outstanding intelligence and her penetrating powers of analysis enabled her to unmask the most carefully concealed workings of capitalist society and in particular of imperialism, even when they were most skilfully disguised, and this gave her something of a tendency – which, incidentally, Marx did not escape either – to overrate the actual effect of the laws of capitalist development so that, with her gift for taking the long-term view, she hoped to speed up this development and thus underestimated the non-capitalist aspects of society in anticipation of their disappearance; this also led her to neglect the question of the peasants.

At the end of his biographical sketch of Rosa Luxemburg, Kautsky wrote: 'Rosa Luxemburg and her friends will always occupy an outstanding position in the history of socialism; but they represent an era that has come to an end.'[325] Our view is the exact opposite; it seems to us that only now, with the failure of social democracy and the crisis of dogmatism, the historical era in which Rosa Luxemburg's thought and method can and must become an intellectual guide for the labour movement is really beginning. Her synthesis of day-to-day struggle and ultimate goal is more than ever necessary to resist the opportunism and revisionism which have reduced the proletariat of the West to abject surrender, as well as the pseudo-Marxist extremism which ignores the essential intermediate steps and wants total revolution 'here and now'. Together with Lenin against whom she waged so many battles, Rosa Luxemburg must once again become better known and appreciated for what she always was: 'the peerless prophet and unforgettable teacher and leader of revolutionary Marxism.'[326]

Appendix

THE German translation from which this English translation has been made is based on Lelio Basso's introduction to his edition of Rosa Luxemburg's political writings, published under the title *Rosa Luxemburg – Scritti politici, (Editori Riuniti, Rome, 1967), as later enlarged and brought up to date for publication in Germany in 1968. Polish sources were all translated from the Italian version.

The abbreviations used for Rosa Luxemburg's works are given below. Also to be consulted are the short bibliographical appendix to O. K. Flechtheim's edition of Rosa Luxemburg's political writing Vol. III, Frankfurt am Main, 1968, and the as yet most complete list of her works, which appears as an appendix to P. Nettl's standard biography of Rosa Luxemburg, published in Cologne in 1968 and which is itself reprinted from a Polish work.

Abbreviations (partial collections and single editions):

(1) Collected works, published by Clara Zetkin and Adolf Warksi, edited by Paul Frölich, Berlin, 1923–1928.
Vol. III *Gegen der Reformismus*, Berlin, 1928.   *GW III.*
Vol. IV *Gewerkschaftkampf und Massenstreik*, Berlin, 1931.   *GW IV.*

(2) Selected Speeches and Writings published by the Marx–Engels–Lenin Institute. 2 Vols., East Berlin, 1951.   *ARS I and II.*

(3) *Wibor Pism.* 2 Vols. Warsaw, 1959.   *WP I and II.*

(4) Political Writings.
Vol. I, published and introduced by O. K. Flechtheim, Frankfurt am Main/Vienna, 1966.   *Pol. Schr. I.*
Vol. II, ditto,   *Pol. Schr II.*
Vol. III, ditto (with bibliography and index of names), 1968.
                                                                Pol. Schr III.

Die Russische Revolution, edited with introduction by O. K. Flechtheim, Frankfurt am Main, 1963, now in *Pol. Schr III*, p. 106 et. seq.   *Russische Revolution.*

Die Akkumulation des Kapitals   *Akkumulation.*
Ein Beitrag zur ökonomischen Erklärung des Imperialismus, Berlin,

1913, and *Antikritik: Die Akkumulation des Kapitals oder Was die
Epigonen aus der Marxschen Theorie gemacht haben.*   *Antikritik.
Eine Antikritik,* Berlin, 1921.
Photostat copy with introduction by Dr. E. März in one vol., Frankfurt
am Main, 1965.
Spartakusbriefe. Published by the *Institut für Marxismus–Leninismus,*
East Berlin, 1958.   *SB.*

The most frequently mentioned periodicals:
Die Neue Zeit, weekly review of the German Social Democratic
Party, 1896–1913, Stuttgart.   *NZ.*
Z pola walki, Zaklad Historii Partii przy   *KC PZPR.*
(From the Battlefield. Organ of the Instititute for the history of the
Polish Communist Party), Warsaw, 1959–1965.

Frequently quoted articles and other shorter works:
Sozialreform oder Revolution?   *Sozialreform.*
Organisationfragen der russischen   *Organisationsfragen.*
Sozialdemokratie
Vorwort zur 'Polnischen Frage'   *Vorwort.*
Massenstreik, Partei und Gewerkschaften   *Massenstreik.*
Reden auf dem Londoner Parteitag der SDAPR   *Reden SDAPR.*
Militarismus, Krieg und Arbeiterklasse   *Militarismus.*
Der Wiederaufbau der Internationale   *Wiederaufbau.*
Die Krise der Sozialdemokratie (with appendix)   *Krise.*
Unser Programm und die politische Situation   *Programm.*

Notes

1. *Notes of a Publicist.* Written at the end of February, 1922, first published 16 April 1924 in *Pravda*, No. 87. In V. I. Lenin, *Selected Works*, Vol 10, p. 313, London, 1936. Lenin's respect for Rosa Luxemburg is shown by the fact that he had many of her works in his library, a catalogue of which has recently been published in Moscow (*Bibliotheco V. I. Lenin v. Kremle*, Moscow, 1960). He had some dozen of her volumes in his study, so they were books that he wished to have easily available. The list also shows the large number of translations of Rosa Luxemburg which were made in Soviet Russia during Lenin's lifetime.
2. Karl Radek, *Rosa Luxemburg, Karl Liebknecht, Leo Jogiches*, p. 25, Hamburg, 1921. This judgement was widely shared at the time; when some letters of Rosa Luxemburg to Mehring were published, the Communist review *The Internationale* wrote that 'she had fertilized the theory of socialism more than anyone since Engels' death.' (*The Internationale*, VI, 1923, 3, p. 67.)
3. Franz Mehring, '*Historisch – materialistische Literatur*' in *Die Neue Zeit*, XXV (1906–07), No. 41, p. 507.
4. George Lukács, '*Geschichte und Klassen-bewusstein.*' *Studien über marxistische Dialektik*, p. 56, Berlin, 1923.
5. cf Paul Frölich, *Rosa Luxemburg, Gedanke und Tat*, p. 348. Frankfurt am Main, 1967. For Rosa Luxemburg's murder, cf also Elisabeth Druck-Hannover and Heinrich Hanover (publishers), '*Der Mord an Rosa Luxemburg und Karl Liebknecht.*' *Dokumentation eines politishen Verbrechens*. Frankfurt am Main, 1967. A detailed account of the trial of the murderers had already been published under the title: *Der Mord an Karl Liebknecht und Rosa Luxemburg: Zusammenfassende Darstellung des gesamten Untersuchungs-materials mit ausführlichem Prozessbericht*, Berlin, 1920.
6. The motions concerning the bolshevization of the Communist parties belonging to the International which were approved at the session of the enlarged executive (March–April, 1925) and published in the periodical *La Correspondance Internationale*, v, 50, still expressly praise 'the greatness of Rosa Luxemburg's works' and describe her as 'a great revolutionary' but consider all her views which deviate from Lenin's as false. His thought was canonized as the sole and universal basis for all the Communist parties and made a dogma. Later on it was stated that theoretical ideas were all the more dangerous where they diverged from Leninism because the author was so close to Leninism. The final condemnation came from Stalin in his letter entitled: 'Concerning certain questions of the history of Bolshevism' to the periodical

Proletarskaia Revolutsia in 1931. (In Rosa Luxemburg, *ARS I*, p. 136, *et seq.*) The expression 'syphilis of the party' was coined by Ruth Fischer (*cf* the speeches of A. Rosenberg and C. Zetkin in *La Correspondance Internationale*, VI, Nos. 35, 36).

Rosa Luxemburg suffered no better fate at the hands of the Social Democrats. It would in fact be difficult to consider the repeated publication of only two of her writings, *Organisationsfragen der russischen Socialdemokratie* and *Die Russische Revolution*, in most cases as anything but a posthumous insult to her, since these two publications were obviously used for anti-communist propaganda and presented completely without reference the general context of her works. As any reader of these works can see, Rosa Luxemburg was not dealing in any definitive or exhaustive way either with Lenin's work or with the Bolshevist revolution, although they contain many valid points which are presented, erroneously, as a sort of definitive condemnation of Leninism by Rosa Luxemburg.

7. 'Sozialreform,' *Pol. Schr. I*, p. 54.

8. This was the scientist speaking, but that side does not represent even half of Marx. For Marx science was an historical, revolutionary driving-force . . . Because Marx was primarily a revolutionary. His real vocation was to contribute, in one way or another, to the overthrow of capitalist society and the State institutions created by that society, to contribute to the emancipation of the modern proletariat which he had been the first to make aware of the conditions of its emancipation – that was his real vocation. (F. Engels, in his speech at Marx's graveside in Highgate cemetery on 17 March 1883, published in *Der Sozialdemokrat*, No. 13 22/3/1883, reprinted in *Marx–Engels Selected Works*, p. 435, London, 1968.)

9. On the evaluation of Marx's conception of revolution, see L. Basser, 'La pluralità delle vie al socialismo nel pensiero di Marx e Engels' in *Mondo Operaio*, 1956, No. 5, and 'Marxismo e democrazia' in *Problemi del socialismo*, 1958, No. 1.

10. There are a number of apologia of Kautsky which were collected and published for his seventieth birthday and his centenary: *Karl Kautsky der Denker und Kämpfer – Festgabe zu seiner siebsigsten Geburtstag*, Vienna, 1924 (articles by W. Ellenbogen, A. Braunthal, H. Bauer, O. Olberg, J. Braunthal, Z. Topalowitch, Z. Ronai, O. Jensen, F. Adler, T. Schlesinger, J. Hannak, R. Abramovitch, A. Bracke, M. Adler, M. Hillquit, F. Brügel), *Karl Kautsky zum 70en Geburtstag*, Berlin 1924 (special number of *Die Gesellschaft*, with contributions by M. Adler, K. Vorländer, A. Braun, Louis B. Boudin, V. Tschernow, E. Bernstein, F. Stampfer, P. Kampffmeyer, J. Marschak, J. Palach, J. Pistiner, J. Sakasoff, J. W. Keto, Th. Dan, B. Nikolaevsky, N. Jordania, R. Seidel, as well as a bibliography of Kautsky's works); *Ein Leben für den Sozialismus – Erinnerungen an Karl Kautsky*, Hanover, 1945 (articles by K. Kautsky, L. Kautsky, F. Adler, F. Stampfer, S. de Wolff,

J. Marschak, Z. Topalovitch, R. Abramovitch, B. Nikolaevsky, N. Jordania, P. Olberg); also: H. Brill, Karl Kautsky, 16 Oct. 1854–17 Oct. 1938 in *Zeitschrift für Politik*, 1954, p. 211, *et seq.*). From a more critical standpoint on the other hand cf the fundamental essay by Karl Korsch, *Die materialistische Geschichtsauffassung. Eine Auseinandersetzung mit Karl Kautsky*, Leipzig, 1929, and more recently Erich Matthias 'Karl Kautsky und der Kautskyanisms' in *Marxismusstudien, Zweite Folge*, Tübingen, 1957.

11. Bernstein himself wrote that Rosa Luxemburg's articles 'were, as far as method goes, amongst the best that were written against me.' *Voraussetzungen des Sozialismus und die Aufgaben der Sozialdemokratie*, p. 178, Stuttgart, 1899, and replying to her in the *Mouvement Socialiste*, 16, 1899, he said that it was not Kautsky, who did not possess Rosa Luxemburg's dialectical ability, but Rosa Luxemburg who had replied to him and she was far more competent, etc. (cf p. 264). Bruno Schönlank also considered her a 'masterly dialectician' or a 'genuine Marx in his prime'. cf Rosa Luxemburg's letter of 17 September 1898 to Leo Jogiches in *Z pola walki*, No. 1, 1962.

12. So orthodox Marxism does not mean uncritical acceptance of the results of Marx's researches, a 'belief' in this or that theory, the exegesis of a 'holy book'. In Marxism, orthodoxy is rather purely a question of method. It is the scientific conviction that in dialectical Marxism the right method of investigation has been discovered and that this method can only be developed, continued and deepened in the way laid down by its founders and that any attempts to transcend it or 'improve' it have led to superficiality, triviality and eclecticism and were bound to do so. (G. Lukács, *op. cit.*, p. 13.)

13. Since Rosa Luxemburg was always pointing out that what was important was not the isolated results of Marx's analysis but his method, we must deal with her writings and teachings likewise. They provide a school for Communism not because of her detailed conclusions but because of her method. (K. Radek, *op. cit.*, p. 25.)

14. 'Massenstreik', *Pol. Schr. I*, p. 39.

15. 'Sozialreform', *Pol. Schr. I*, p. 126.

16. The decisive difference between Marxism and bourgeois science is not the predominance of economic motives in the explanation of historical events but the viewpoint of totality. The category of totality, the universal and decisive predominance of the whole over the parts, is the essence of the method which Marx took over from Hegel and in his own original way made into the basis of a completely new science . . . And what is basically revolutionary in proletarian science is not only the fact that its content is

revolutionary in opposition to bourgeois science but first and foremost that its method is essentially revolutionary. It is the predominance of the category of totality which represents the revolutionary principle in science. (G. Lukács, *op. cit.*, p. 39.)

17. 'Sozialreform', *Pol. Schr. I*, p. 125.
18. *ibid.* p. 87.

19. If however we consider these phenomena apart from the historical context which produced them and turn them into abstract models of absolute and universal validity, we are committing the greatest sin against the 'Holy Spirit' of Marxism, that is, against his dialectical–historical way of thinking. ('Organisationsfragen', *Pol. Schr. III*, pp. 96, 97.)

20. *ARS II*, p. 525.

21. So the very idea of that modest, virtuous patriotic defensive war that our members of Parliament and editors have in mind today is a pure fiction which leaves out any historical conception of totality and its world-wide implications. ('Krise', *Pol. Schr. II*, p. 122.)

22. *ibid.* p. 124.
23. 'Organisationsfragen', *Pol. Schr. III*, p. 83.
24. P. Frölich, *op. cit.* pp. 37, 38; *cf* also K. Radek, *op. cit.* p. 4: 'The way in which she poses the problem of the social revolution is unique in socialist literature.'
25. The review *Sprawa Robotnicza* (The Cause of the Worker) was founded in Zürich in 1893. The editors were Rosa Luxemburg, Leo Tyszka (Jogiches), Adolf Warski and Julian Marchlevski (Karski). It immediately became the official organ of the SDKP (Social Democrats of the Kingdom of Poland), when the latter was founded in the same year by the same people. (Report on the Third International Socialist Labour Congress in Zürich, 1893, concerning the state and development of the social democratic movement in Russian Poland from 1889 to 1893, drawn up by the editors of the review *Sprawa Robotnicza*, the organ of the Social Democrats of the Kingdom of Poland.)
26. Report to the International Socialist Labour and Trade Union Congress in London on the social democratic movement in Russian Poland 1893–1896.
27. *ARS II*, pp. 28, 29.
28. *ARS II*, p. 33.

29. For M. Proudhon every economic category has two sides, a good one and a bad one. He considers categories as the petty bourgeois considers great historical figures. *Napoleon* is a great man, he did a lot of good but he also did a lot of bad things. The *good side* and the *bad side*, the *advantages* and *disadvantages* taken together constitute the contradiction in every economic category. (Karl

Marx, 'The Poverty of Philosophy', in *Marx–Engels Works*, Vol. 4, p. 131.)

30. The programme of the Spartakus League is in deliberate opposition to the attitude hitherto adopted by the Erfurt programme, in deliberate contrast to the separation into immediate so-called minimum demands for the political and economic struggle from the maximum programme of the ultimate goal of socialism. ('Program', *Pol Schr. II*, p. 181.)

31. G. Lukács, *op. cit.* pp. 36, 37.

32. 'Sozialreform', *Pol. Schr. I*, pp. 130, 131. Rosa Luxemburg was quick to point out that a similar contradiction is also revealed in the isolated aspects of the struggle, eg

The role of social democracy in bourgeois legislative bodies is beset with inner contradictions from the start. Taking part in positive legislation, with practical results if possible and at the same time adopting a position of fundamental opposition to the capitalist State at every turn – that is the general outline of the difficult task facing our own parliamentary representatives. ('Nachbetrachtungen zum Parteitag', in *Sächsische Arbeiterzeitung*, 14 October 1898, reprinted in *GW III*, p. 157.)

33. cf 'Organisationsfragen', *Pol. Schr. III*, pp. 103 *et seq*.

34. 'Sozialreform', *Pol. Schr. I*, p. 99.

35. 'Massenstreik', *Pol. Schr. I*, p. 210.

36. The special quality of Rosa Luxemburg's fight against revisionism lies in the fact that she vigorously brought its social political content into the open and so waged her struggle not on the plane of subtle theory but as a fight against a practical bourgeois trend in the labour movement. Her merciless fight against revisionism, her biting irony, the vigour of her attack were all attributed to her volcanic revolutionary temperament. This is a completely superficial judgement. Rosa Luxemburg knew the history of the international labour movement better than almost anyone. For her it was never a mere collection of stories taken from the lives and theories of the founders of the various socialist systems. The history of the international labour movement showed her that ideological struggles inside the labour movement always had an underlying social basis and that conflicts over methods and tactics were always struggles for ascendency by one group over others inside the labour movement, with opportunism always represented by that section of the working class which was closest to the bourgeoisie. Rosa Luxemburg detected that revisionism not only corresponded to a practice of bourgeois elements that had been attracted to the party after the abolition of anti-socialist legislation in Germany, and after their parliamentary successes in France and Italy but also to the policy of large sections of the working classes

who had been lifted on the wave of economic prosperity and was beginning to become integrated into bourgeois society. (Karl Radek, *op. cit* p. 13.) But [opportunism] is much worse than wrong; it is completely and utterly un-social-democratic. It is not the mistaken idea of a Social Democrat. It is the correct idea of a bourgeois democrat who mistakenly imagines himself to be a Social Democrat. (Rosa Luxemburg, 'Nachbetrachtungen', *GW III*, p. 159.)

37. 'Organisationsfragen', *Pol. Schr. III*, p. 103. As we know, Lenin considered opportunism as the specific expression of a particular section of society, a workers' aristocracy. So it is not true that Lenin thought that the labour movement could be protected once and for all against opportunist deviations; but he certainly looked upon it as a phenomenon whose roots within the movement were purely marginal, that is to say to be found amongst privileged minorities and so more a necessary dialectical factor in the movement as a whole than the reflection of the contradictions in capitalist society, as Rosa Luxemburg thought. It is clear that even for Rosa Luxemburg, opportunism as representing the side of the movement turned towards the present would occur more easily in those sections better satisfied with present conditions, that is to say, amongst workers' aristocracies: yet it still lurks as a constant hidden danger for the whole movement, as it were a recurring temptation at any and every moment, capable of erupting and spreading throughout the whole or almost the whole of the working classes. The history of the western European labour movement would seem to have confirmed Rosa Luxemburg's thesis and it appears to us theoretically more correct.

38. 'Sozialreform', *Pol. Schr. I*, p. 132. It is unnecessary to draw the reader's attention to the fact that at the time this work was written, the words 'social democracy' and 'social democratic' had not yet taken on the specific meaning of opportunist revisionism which they now have; at that time they meant rather the Marxist inspired labour movement. Even Lenin's party, the future Communist Party, was at that time called the Social Democratic Labour Party of Russia.

39. If one wing of the party had always had a propensity to under-rate or even to deny the value of positive day-to-day action, the flourishing expansion of the movement since 1890 was bound to lead to the opposite extreme, the overestimation of the positive work of reform and opportunist trends. The party congress in Erfurt represented the typical moment of transition when the party had to fight on two fronts. (Rosa Luxemburg, 'Nachbetrachtungen', *GW III*, p. 151.)

40. 'Zum kommenden Parteitag' in *Leipziger Volkzeitung*, 15 September 1899, reprinted in *GW III*, p. 172.
41. *ibid.* pp. 172, 173.
42. Rosa Luxemburg knew very well, especially after her early

militant years in the German Social Democratic Party, that opportunism was also to be found amongst those who did not consider
themselves as such but looked upon themselves as radicals.

More than once during the debates on foreign policy she re-
proached the most prominent amongst the leaders of the Social
Democratic Party with never doing what they said; and she particularly pointed out that when it was a question of voting for
socialist resolutions, they showed themselves strongly radical, but
when they found themselves actually forced to fight against war
and the government which was provoking it, all their radicalism
seemed to evaporate. At that time, such words seemed incredibly
bold: the German Social Democratic Party of the time was at the
height of its glory.

cf the speech by Zinoviev to the Petrograd Soviet in *Karl Liebknecht
et Rosa Luxemburg – Discours prononcé par G. Zinoviev et L. Trotsky
à la réunion du Soviet de Petrograd le 18 janvier, 1919, Editions de
l'Internationale Communiste*, p. 19, Petrofrad, 1919.

43. 'Sozialreform', *Pol. Schr I*, p. 128.
44. 'Zum Kommenden Parteitag', *op. cit. GW III*, p. 178.
45. *ibid.* p. 180. After the success of the reformists at the Milan party
congress of the Italian socialists and on the eve of the Reggio nell'
Emilia Party Congress, she wrote once again on the subject of so called
'practical politics':

A few years of this 'practical politics' have shown it to be the
worst possible because it is intent on cutting off the branch on
which it is sitting. It loses contact with the masses, loses its foot-
hold, becomes the plaything of bourgeois policy and drags
syndicalism, that anarchistic caricature of revolutionary socialism,
down with it, as a shadow of its own weakness. Yet this experiment
which socialist opportunism has conducted with such inexorable
logic can have only one result for Italy, the regeneration of the
labour movement. (Rinascenza Socialista', in *La Soffitta*, Rome,
15 May 1911.)

46. I think that the intentions of Schweitzer and so on are honest
intentions but they are *Realpolitiker*. They want to accommodate
themselves to existing circumstances and not surrender this
privilege of 'real politics' to the exclusive use of Herr Miquel and
Co. . . . So they want to take the circumstances as they are and not
irritate the government, just like our *republican* 'real politicians'
who are willing to 'put up with' a Hohenzollern emperor. As
I'm not a *Realpolitiker* I have found it necessary to sever all
connections with the *Sozialdemokrat* in a public declaration
signed by myself and Engels. (K. Marx, Letter to Kugelmann,
23 February 1865, in *Letters to Dr Kugelmann*, p. 31, Martin
Lawrence.)

47. Preface to *Die polnische Frage und die sozialistische Bewegung*. Italian translation from the Polish text in *Rosa Luxemburg, Scritti politici. A cura di Lelio Basso*, p. 265, Rome, 1967.

48. *Die industrielle Entwickling Polens*, Leipzig, 1898.

49. Letter of 15 August 1898, published in *Z pola walki*, Warsaw, 1959, No. I (5), p. 72. From Italian translation in Lelio Basso (editor), *op. cit.* p. 41.

50. 'Sozialreform', *Pol. Schr. I*, p. 91.

51. *Was die Epigonen aus der Marxschen Theorie gemacht haben. Eine Antikritik*, p. 37, Leipzig, 1921. In fact, the writer is here referring to an objective necessity which she took from her theory of accumulation.

52. 'Sozialreform', *Pol. Schr. I*, p. 101.

53. *Antikritik, op. cit.* p. 117.

54. 'Erörterungen, äber die Taktik' in *Sächschishe Arbeiterzeitung*, 13 October 1898, reprinted in *GW III*, p. 163.

55. 'Sozialreform', *Pol. Schr. I*, p. 75.

56. 'Organisationsfragen', *Pol. Schr. III*, p. 92.

57. 'Die Russische Revolution', *Pol. Schr. III*, p. 113.

58. *ibid.* p. 106.

59. 'Wiederaufbau', *op. cit. ARS II*, p. 527.

60. *ibid.* p. 519.

61. Preface, *op. cit.* p. 44.

62. 'Wiederanfbau', *op. cit. ARS II*, p. 528.

63. *ibid.* pp. 530, 531.

64. *ibid.* p. 519.

65. 'Organisationsfragen', *Pol. Schr. III*, p. 85. The statement that Russian socialism had been given the task of 'replacing a section of the historical process by conscious intervention' is in our opinion very important in order to understand the imbalances and difficulties following the October Revolution, when this intention assumed giant proportions. For the implications and consequences of this interpretation of the role of the labour movement and the party, *cf* L. Basso *Da Stalin a Kruschov*, Milan, 1962. A similar conception is to be found in V. I. Lenin, *State and Revolution, op. cit* 1937, Vol 7, p. 71. 'The Russian workers . . . carried over . . . as it were more rapidly on to the fresh soil of our labour movement, the rich experience of the more advanced neighbouring country.'

66. Speech at the London Party Congress of the *SDAPR, ARS I*, p. 287.

67. Absolutism [in Russia] cannot be mentioned at any arbitrarily chosen moment as if only sufficient 'effort' and 'perseverance' are required. The collapse of absolutism is merely the outward expression of the inner social and class development of Russian Society. ('Massenstreik', *Pol. Schr. I*, p. 159.)

68. Rosa Luxemburg is here taking over the well known statement of Marx at the beginning of his *18th Brumaire*:

They make their own history but then do not make it just as they please; they do not make it under circumstances chosen by themselves but under circumstances directly encountered, given and transmitted from the past.

But whereas Marx at that time placed the emphasis on pre-existing circumstances, that is to say on what is objectively given which weights 'like an incubus on the brain of the living', R. L. emphasizes the subjective factor, that is to say, men's action. So we are here in no way dealing with a mechanistic and deterministic interpretation of Marxism.

69. 'Krise', *Pol. Schr. II*, p. 30.
70. *ibid*. p. 147.
71. 'Die Krise in Frankreich', in *Sächsische Arbeiterzeitung*, 29.10.1898, reprinted in *GW III*, p. 269.
72. 'Krise', *Pol. Schr. II*, p. 147.
73. P. Frölich, *op. cit.* p. 10.
74. 'Was will der Spartakusbund?', *Pol. Schr. II*, p. 159.
75. 'Programme', *Pol. Schr. II*, p. 181.
76. 'Massenstreik', *Pol. Schr. I*, p. 205.
77. 'Organisationsfragen', *Pol. Schr. III*, p. 89.
78. Preface, *op. cit.* p. 265.
79. 'Massenstreik', *Pol. Schr. I*, p. 137.
80. Rede SDAPR', *ARS II*, p. 286.
81. 'Antikritik', p. 114.

82. She never stopped warning the masses: 'A world war is approaching!' She explained to them why neither the Dual nor the Triple Alliance were instruments of peace but instruments of war. She told them . . . that it was the task of the party to enlighten the masses as to the true state of affairs and fill them with self-knowledge. Then the hour will soon strike when workers and soldiers will refuse to take part in the crime of war. (Henriette Roland-Holst van der Schalk, *Rosa Luxemburg, Ihr Leben und Wirken*, pp. 120, 121. Zürich, 1937.)

83. 'Krise', *Pol. Schr II*, p. 144.
84. Preface, *op. cit.* p. 265.
85. 'Sozialreform', *Pol. Schr. I*, p. 81.

86. Napoleon once said: 'Two factors decide the outcome of a battle: the earthly factor, that is the terrain, the quality of the equipment, atmospheric conditions, etc., and the "heavenly" factor, that is to say the morale of the army, its enthusiasm, its belief in its own cause.' The "earthly" factor in the present war is being mainly looked after by the Essen firm of Krupp on the German side and the "heavenly" is primarily the concern of the Social Democrats. ('Wiederaufbau', *ARS II*, p. 519.)

146 ROSA LUXEMBURG: A REAPPRAISAL

87. *Akkumulation des Kapitals*, p. 430. Berlin, 1913.
88. *Antikritik*, pp. 13, 14.

89. The typical outward phenomena of the imperialistic period: the competition between capitalist States for colonies and spheres of influence, investment opportunities for European capital, the system of international loans, militarism, protectionism, the predominant role of banks and industrial cartels in international politics, are now universally known. Their connection with the last phase of capitalist development and their significance for the accumulation of capital are so blatant that they are known and acknowledged by both the upholders and the opponents of capitalism. But social democracy cannot remain content with this empirical knowledge. It must discover the exact form of the economic laws governing the relationships between these phenomena and lay bare the real roots of this great complex of imperialistic manifestations since, *as always in such cases, only the precise theoretical understanding of the roots of the problems can provide even our practical struggle against imperialism with the necessary certainty, clearsightedness and vigour required by a proletarian policy. (Antikritik*, p. 21. Italics by Lelio Basso.)

90 *Akkumulation*, p. 392.
91. *ibid.* p. 423.
92. 'Krise', *Pol. Schr. II*, p. 119.
93. The means of production of which Rosa Luxemburg is thinking is above all the labour force which is forcibly dragged into the orbit of capitalist production in the remotest corner of the earth.
94. *Akkumulation*, p. 329.
95. 'Sozialreform', *Pol. Schr. I*, p. 78.
96. *ibid.* p. 79.
97. *Akkumulation*, p. 436.
98. *ibid*, p. 444.
99. Though the Social Democrats were reluctant to accept Rosa Luxemburg's analysis of the economic function of rearmament, the capitalists were very conscious of this function.

On 3 December 1901, the President of the *Deutscher Flottenverein*, Prince Salm-Horstmar, sent Admiral Tirpitz a letter drawing his attention to the fact that in view of the poor state of the economy and the unfavourable trade and industrial situation, a number of persons representing various party trends had asked him to urge that the naval programme should be accelerated; a most important factor would be to commission new warships and so revive trade and industry and this would bring about an improvement on the Stock Exchange, helping many shares and strengthening the market. (W. G. Hallgarten, *Vorkriegs–Imperialismus*, p. 164. Paris, 1935.)

100. *Akkumulation*, p. 445.
101. *ibid.* 424.
102. *Antikritik*, p. 118. It is not necessary to point out that Rosa Luxemburg was making her observations before the appearance of a strongly organized system of socialist States, let alone of atomic weapons. This does not alter the fact that there is still a strong dose of Utopianism, even if the fight is politically justified.
103. *ibid.* p. 120.
104. The fundamental criticism of Rosa Luxemburg's conception of imperialism on the political level (we are not considering the economic aspect) is that she postulates that at a given moment capitalism will become impossible and socialism will thus become inevitable. In fact, it is one thing to outline a certain trend of historical development and quite another to base your own political prophecies on the assumption that this trend will be realized. In his controversy with Kautsky over the ultra-imperialistic stage of capitalism, Lenin admits the truth of Kautsky's hypothesis that

> the *trend* of development is towards the creation of one single world trust comprising every enterprise and every State without exception. But this trend takes place in such circumstances so rapidly, and with such contradictions, conflicts and upheavals – and not only economic but also political and national, etc. – that unfailing, even *before* the stage of a single world trust is reached, of an 'ultra-imperialist' world union of all national capital investment, imperialism must inevitably collapse, and capitalism turn into its opposite. (Preface to N. Bukharin's pamphlet: *World Economics and Imperialism*.)

Even Rosa Luxemburg, after having established that, economically, an unlimited development of the accumulation of capital was impossible, added:

> Naturally, that does not mean such reservations, which are part of any Marxist's ABC, are nevertheless always indispensable, as we shall see, to our 'experts' – that the historical process must or even can go to the extreme limit of this economic impossibility. The objective trend of the evolution of capitalism towards that end is enough to sharpen the contradictions within society to such an extent, both politically and socially, and to lead to such an unbearable situation as to bring about the end of the prevailing system. (*Antikritik*, p. 37.) And later: 'Can this moment ever really come? Let us not forget that it is only a theoretical fiction, precisely because the accumulation of capital is not only an economic but a political process . . . Here as elsewhere in history, theory completely fulfils its function only by showing us the *trend* of a development, the logical conclusion towards which it is leading. This conclusion itself can never be reached, any more than any

other earlier period of historical development has been able to reach its logical consequences. It is the less *necessary* for it to reach it because social consciousness, incorporated this time in the socialist proletariat, intervenes more actively as a factor in the blind interplay of forces.' (*ibid.* pp. 916, 117.)

And for this reason, Rosa Luxemburg was right in rejecting this criticism, which was raised against her particularly by Otto Bauer, not only by drawing attention to the exact meaning and wording of her arguments but also to her practical opposition to war, whereas, while calling down on her the 'growing revolt of the steadily ascending working classes, educated, united and organized by the very mechanism of the productive process of capitalism' her critic had entrenched himself in a quietist policy of impotent centrism like Kautsky at the very moment when the hour had come for the masses to revolt.

105. According to E. Matthias (*op. cit.*) the theoretical part, although containing the proof of the future advent of socialism, albeit couched in evolutionary rather than in Marxist terms, was basically intended to sustain the enthusiasm of the masses and so bind them to the party which, in practice, was only concerned with day-to-day politics, in fact, a sort of substitute paradise for believers.

106. F. Engels, 'Der Sozialismus in Deutschland', in *NZ X* (1891–1892), I, No. 19, p. 580.

107. *Protokoll uber die Verhandlungen des Parteitags der Soziadem-kratischen Partei Deutschlands. Abgehalten zu Erfurt vom 14 his 20 Oktober, 1891*, p. 172. And earlier we read: 'We [need] only to wait for the moment when we have to take over the power as it falls from [bourgeois society's] hands.'

108. 'Der neue Reichstag', in *NZ XI* (1892–1893), 2, p. 452.

109. Karl Kautsky, *Der Parlamentarismus, die Volksgesetzgebung and die Sozialdemokratie*, Stuttgart, 1893.

110. These speeches were published as a pamphlet under a title which referred expressly to the immediate tasks: *Über die nächsten Aufgaben der deutschen Soziul–demokratie. Zwei Reden gehalten am 1 Juni und 6 Juli am 'Eldorado' zu München*. Munich, 1891.

111. Gerhard A. Ritter, *Die Arbeiterbewegung im Wilhelmischen Reich*, p. 187. Berlin, 1959.

112. H. Müller, *Der Klassenkampf in der deutschen Sozialdemokratie*, p. 25. Zürich, 1892.

113. *Protokoll des dritten Kongresses der Gewerkschaften Deutsch-lands, abgehalten zu Frankfurt am Main von 8 bis 13 Mai 1899*, p. 113. Hamburg.

114. G. A. Ritter (*op. cit.* p. 160, note 68) mentions that at the meeting of the free union of woodworkers in Göttingen, one speaker specifically said: 'Since the future State cannot be expected to materialize overnight, we are in duty bound to remain ready to defend ourselves

in present conditions.' cf also in the letter of 8 September 1903 from Adler to Bebel in V. Adler, *Briefwechsel*, p. 421, the reference to the increasing tendency amongst the workers 'to settle down quietly to enjoy their gains, to be able to live like everyone else.'

115. Thus official prewar German social democracracy, as represented by August Bebel, combined strong social political activity with a passive formal radicalism in all other spheres of public life. The average social democratic official had no real connection with problems of foreign policy, military matters, education, justice, government administration, even with the economy in general and especially with agrarian problems. He did not think that one day the time would come when he, as a Social Democrat, would have to take decisions on all these matters. What was close to his heart was everything connected with the professional interests of the worker in industry in the narrow sense. Here he was an expert and active. In addition, he was perhaps most interested in the question of the right to vote. (A. Rosenberg, *Geschichte der Weimarer Republik*, p. 12. Frankfurt, 1961.)

116. E. Bernstein, 'Ignaz Auer, der Führer, Freund und Berater', in *Sozialistische Monatshefte*, I, pp. 345, 346. 1907.

117. As early as 1890, at the Party Congress in Halle, Bebel had pointed out that nine-tenths of the work of the party was directed to raising and improving the standard of living of the workers 'within the framework of the present bourgeois order of society.' *Protokoll über die Verhandlungen des Parteitags der Sozialdemokratischen Partei Deutschlands. Abgehalten zu Halle a.S. vom 12 bis 18 Oktober 1890*, p. 102. Berlin, 1890; and when Vollmar was criticized for stating that the party must stop discussing tomorrow and concentrate all its forces on the most immediate and urgent matters, he had some justification in replying that he had merely drawn attention to the policy that the party had, in fact, long been practising.

118. H. Roland-Holst, *op. cit* p. 75. cf also A. Krajevski's introduction to Rosa Luxemburg's letter to Leo Jogiches in *Z pola walki*, nos. 11, 12, p. 178. 1931.

119. F. Tych, introduction to the publication of Rosa Luxemburg's letters to Leo Jogiches in *Z pola walki*, No. 3, p. 128. 1961. cf also P. Frölich, *op. cit.* p. 60. The German leaders' distrust and also dislike of Rosa Luxemburg is expressed even in their letters: cf for example V. Adler, *Briefwechsel*, p. 513.

120. J. P. Nettl, the author of the most recent and comprehensive biography of Rosa Luxemburg, writes that opportunism in the Second International was partly her discovery. (*Rosa Luxemburg*, p. 853. London, 1966.)

121. Rosa Luxemburg's letter to Robert Seidl, the first dated 23 June 1898, the second undated (1903), published in *Z pola walki*, 1959, No. 1,

pp. 69, 84, V. also parts of the second letter in P. Frölich, *op. cit.* pp. 58, 59.
122. Letter to H. Roland-Holst of 17 December 1904, in H. Roland-Holst, *op. cit.* pp. 215, 216.
123. Letter to Clara Zetkin, early in 1907, reprinted in P. Frölich, *op. cit.* pp. 156, 157. Also Rosa Luxemburg's harsh judgement on the social democratic leaders in a letter written in prison to Mathilde Wurm on 28 December 1916.

> Even thinking of your gallery of heroes gives me a pain in the neck: sickly Haase, Dittmann with his lovely beard and lovely speeches in the Reichstag, Kautsky the wandering shepherd whom your Emmo [Emmanuel Wurm, L.B.] of course follows through thick and thin, magnificent Arthur [Stadthagen] *ah, je n'en finirai plus!* I promise you I'd sooner be shut up here for years and years rather than 'fight' (forgive the expression!) together with your heroes or even to have anything to do with them at all! (*Briefe an Freunde*, p. 45. Hamburg, 1950.)

As for her judgement on Kautsky's evolutionary optimism, it is interesting to compare two letters written at an interval of several years. On 11 July 1900, she wrote to Jogiches:

> My discussion with K.K. naturally dealt with the general situation in the party (opportunism), its future and the tactics to be pursued. I shall be able to tell you all this better by word of mouth: his ideas can be summed up in the saying of Ben Akiba: everything has always existed, so there's no point in worrying about it; material progress leads to socialism, so everything will be all right and so on and so forth. (*Z pola walki*, 3, p. 167. 1964.)

And on 15 April 1917, writing from prison to Luisa Kautsky, she spoke of 'a comfortable fatalistic optimism which serves to hide his own impotence, that's what I hate in your revered "spouse".' W. Blumenberg, *Einige Briefe Rosa Luxemburgs*, in *International Review of Social History*, 1, p. 103. 1963. It is worth emphasizing the acuteness of her judgement at a time when Lenin himself still believed in Bebel's and Kautsky's revolutionary spirit. *cf.* Lenin on Bebel in *Trade Union Neutrality* reprinted in V. I. Lenin, *On Trade Unions*, p. 205. Moscow, 1970. The judgement of history can only confirm Rosa Luxemburg's view that the leaders of the Social Democratic Party, starting with Bebel, while vocal opponents of reformism, in reality only used revolutionary terminology in order to hide their reformist policies. The internal strife within the party which lasted for a whole decade from 1898 onwards never went as deep as it seemed, and had basically no influence on the practical policies of the Social Democratic Party. On the one hand, the willingness of the revisionists to meet the existing order half-way was considerably hampered by the social structure of the German Empire and on the other the radical majority, with Bebel in the lead, represented within these very limitations, the same desire for social and political reform as was openly expressed by the minority. In general, therefore, the conflict became merely that 'one side approved as reformist what the other side also advocated but described as revolutionary.' E. Matthias, *op. cit.* p. 167.

124. 'Krise', *Pol. Schr. II*, p. 22.

125. C. E. Schorske, *German Social Democracy 1905–1917*, p. 43. Cambridge (Mass.), 1955.

126. Our egregious comrade seems not to possess the slightest inkling of the existence of a single particular direction of social development in every country. On the contrary, he looks on history as an obliging salesgirl who picks out from the mass of goods in her shop something for everyone according to their taste and desires and the socialists ought naturally to ask for the best things because they come into the shop with their mandate of future lords of the world. ('Zur Taktik der polnischen Sozialdemokratie', in *Vorwärts*, 25 July 1896.)

127. *ibid.*

128. The proletariat is not all-powerful; its whole power consists in realizing the revolutionary part of the trend of capitalist development. ('Nacjonalism a socialdemokracja rosykska i polska: 1 Socjalpatriotyczna robinsonada' in *Przeglad Socjaldemokratyczny (Socialdemocratic Observer)*, 1903, No. 10.)

129. 'Socjalpatriotyczne lamance programmowe', *ibid.* 1902, No. 3.

130. In a letter to Marta Rosenbaum written in prison in April 1917, she attacked the party from whom 'in the deathly quiet preceding the war, impatience [was] the greatest virtue, but unfortunately too little practised'. *Briefe an Freunde*, pp. 159, 160.

131. 'Krise', *Pol. Schr. II*, p. 24.

132. Speech in the general assembly of the Free Trade Unions in Hagen, 1 October 1910, reprinted in *ARS II*, pp. 360, 361.

133. 'Sozialreform', *Pol. Schr. I*, p. 86.

134. 'Massenstreik', *Pol. Schr. I*, p. 199.

135. 'Sozialreform', *Pol. Schr. I*, p. 83.

136. 'Erörterungen über die Taktik', *op. cit. GW III*, p. 164.

137. In his book *Der Weg zur Macht*, Kautsky took up the expression 'a labour of Sisyphus' and the trade union organ the *Korrespondenzblatt* for its part published a series of articles refuting this theory. This series was later published separately under the title *Sisyphusarbeit oder positive Erfolge?* (Berlin, 1910). For this whole controversy cf Frölich *Einleitung zu GW IV*.

138. 'Massenstreik', *Pol. Schr. I*, pp. 210, 211.

139. *ibid.* p. 213. Rosa Luxemburg's comments must of course be seen against the background of the period when they were written. Today

the trade unions have a far wider range of responsibilities but the task of political leadership still belongs to the party.

140. 'Und zum drittenmal das Belgische Experiment', in *NZ XX* (1901–1902), 2, No. 35, pp. 275, 276.

141. *ibid* p. 276.

142. 'Massenstreik', *Pol. Schr. I*, pp. 210, 211.

143. 'Die badische Budgetabstimmung (1910)', in *Bremer Bürger-zeitung*, August 1910, reprinted in *GW III*, p. 454.

144. 'Massenstreik', *Pol. Schr. I*, p. 163.

145. 'Was nun?', in *Gleichheit*, 5 February 1912, reprinted in *GW III*, p. 526.

146. Our real victory and our real power lie in the four and a half million voters . . . and it is purely the pressure of these masses from outside which gives our parliamentary group its weight in the Reichstag, whether the group has twenty members more or less. ('Unsere Stichwahltaktik' in *Leipziger Volkszeitung*, 4 March 1912, reprinted in *GW III*, p. 509.)

In this form, this statement may sound exaggerated and wrong, but its meaning is clear in the context: the twenty additional deputies had had to be gained by alliances and agreements which sacrificed socialist aims and obscured class consciousness by weakening the spirit of aggression and the strength of the party. cf also in 'Was weiter?', *Dortmunder Arbeiterzeitung*, 14–15 March 1910, reprinted in *GW IV*, p. 509:

It is impossible for the question of electoral reform in Prussia to be settled by parliamentary means: only immediate mass action in the country can bring about a change here.

147. But what struggle, what action, what purely economic strike does not carry some risk for the activist organizations of the workers? If the powerful organization of our German trade unions and their numerical strength were to be a reason for our trade unions to be more careful about taking such risks in its actions than weaker trade unions in other countries, as for example in Sweden or in Italy, then this would be a dangerous argument against the trade unions themselves. For this would lead to the strange conclusion that the bigger and stronger our organizations are, the less capable of action and the more timid we become . . . The very purpose of a strong organization of the trade unions would come under question, since we need organization as a means to an end, as arms for our struggle and not as an end in itself. (*ibid.* pp. 515, 516.)

148. In reply to the article 'Was weiter?' (*op. cit.*) which, after being rejected by the official party organ *Vorwärts* and the theoretical periodical *Neue Zeit*, was published in the *Dortmunder Arbeiter-*

zeitung, Kautsky wrote an article in the *Neue Zeit* entitled 'Was nun?' in which he borrowed from the military studies of Delbrück the idea of a strategy of attrition, which would lead to victory by tiring an enemy out as opposed to a 'strategy of overthrowing' which instead sets out to crush the enemy, and put forward the view that for the class struggle in Germany the first type was more appropriate than the second. In her turn Rosa Luxemburg reacted to this conception, which was remarkably well suited to justifying the quietist tactics of the Social Democrats (which were inevitably to lead to their surrender 4 August 1914) in an article entitled 'Ermattung oder Kampf?' which was published in the *Neue Zeit* on 27 May and 3 June.

149. 'Sozialreform', *Pol. Schr. I*, pp. 108, 109.

150. *ibid.* p. 110.

151. *ibid.* pp. 118, 119.

152. *Nacjonalism a socjaldemokracja, op. cit.*

153. cf also the speech at the London Congress of the SDAPR, *ARS II*, p. 274.

154. 'Sozialreform', *Pol. Schr. I*, p. 53.

155. This possibility was, of course, not unknown to both Marx and Engels also:

> The solution will not begin to be realized until, as the result of a world war, the proletariat finds itself projected into the leading role in the country which dominates the world markets – England. The revolution which finds here not its end but merely its organizational beginning is no short-lived revolution. (*Class Struggles in France, 1848–1850*, p. 114. London.)

Engels, too, in his introduction to S. Borkheim's pamphlet *Zur Erinnerung für die deutschen Mordpatrioten, 1806–1807* had also foreseen that the next war was bound to be a European war, which within the space of two or three years would cause the same amount of devastation as the Thirty Years' War, would disorganize industry, trade and credit, create conditions leading to universal bankruptcy, cause the downfall of the old States, etc.

> It is absolutely impossible to foresee how it will all end and who will emerge victorious: only one result is absolutely certain: general exhaustion and the establishment of the conditions necessary for the ultimate triumph of the working classes.

Even during the Crimean War, Marx and Engels had hoped that it would create the conditions required for a revolution. However, they had always considered a crisis as the more likely eventuality and the International Congress in London in 1898 referred in an official motion to economic crisis as the cause of revolution; and this was the accepted doctrine of everyone who believed in the socialist revolution.

156. The last decade of the nineteenth century saw the conclusion of the Franco–Russian Alliance in 1891, leading to the polarization of the

forces of Europe into the Triple Alliance and the Dual Alliance, the active entry into the imperialistic struggle of Japan (her war with China in 1894–1895), of the United States (Mackinley's election in 1896 and the sugar war with Spain in 1898), Italy's attack on Abyssinia (1896) and England's on the Boers (1899); the tension between France and England in Africa reached its culmination in the Fachoda incident and Germany's struggle with England for naval supremacy began under Kaiser Wilhelm II's instigation. But very few people recognized these phenomena as marking the beginning of a new phase of capitalism which contained within itself the 'historical necessity' of the World War. Rosa Luxemburg herself provided her interpretation as early as 8 January 1899 in a letter to Jogiches:

> In international politics in the last five or six years, the principal part was played by Constantinople, round which the whole international struggle centred. And since this was only a matter of acquiring a purely strategic point, in the last ten years the policy of supporting Turkey's integrity by a political balance of power was created. Thereby the *problem* of Constantinople reached a state of suspended animation where the development of international relations came to a full stop. Around 1895 an important change took place: the Japanese war opened up the Chinese door and European policy, urged on by capitalist and State interests, hastily turned towards Asia. Here the international struggle and the policies connected with it had a wide field of operations, the occupation and division of the whole of Asia became the aim of European policy. Asia is very quickly being taken over bit by bit and now Persia and Afghanistan too are being attacked by Russia and England respectively. This is giving fresh impetus to the European conflicts in Africa and the struggle has broken out with renewed vigour (Fachoda, Delagoa, Madagascar). It is clear that the partition of Asia and Africa is the furthermost objective beyond which European policies will no longer have very much scope for further development. Then, as recently in the Eastern question, there will be a parenthesis and the European States will have nothing left to do except hurl themselves on each other until the moment of final political crisis arrives. (Z pola walki, 1903, Nos. 1, 2.)

157. At the Mainz Party Congress of 1900, Ledebour, also representing the left, had defined imperialism in the words later taken over by Lenin, as 'the final stage of capitalism'. The world imperialism was not in current use at that time and the expression 'world policy' was more common. Ledebour had spoken of the 'new era of the policy of spoliation and oppression of peoples' which was represented by Chamberlain in England and Mackinley in America and added:

> 'We (are dealing) with phenomena of world historical importance in the last stage of capitalism.' Speaking previously, however,

Fendrich from Karlsruhe had stated that 'we are facing, perhaps the last, stage of development (*Entwicklungsstufe*) of capitalism'. (*Protokoll über die Verhandlungen des Parteitags der Sozialdemokratischen Partei Deutschlands. Abgehalten zu Mainz vom 17 bis 21 September 1900*, pp. 166, 167. Berlin, 1900.)

158. *Compte rendu sténographique non-officiel da la version française du cinquième Congrès Socialiste international tenu à Paris du 23 au 27 septembre 1900*, pp. 181–185. Paris, 1901. Very few historians have emphasized the importance and originality of the contribution that this report of Rosa Luxemburg's made and the prospects it opened up. cf however the correct assessment by G. A. Ritter, *op. cit.* pp. 195, 196.

159. *Internationaler Sozialisten – Kongress, Stuttgart 1907 vom 18 bis 24 August*, Berlin 1907, p. 97. Later on, when writing the history of the attitudes adopted under the Second Internationale, Zinoviev, at that time Lenin's right hand man in Switzerland and co-editor of the central organ of the Bolshevist Party, said that this speech was the only one made in Stuttgart that diverged in principle from the French and German standpoint on which the matters under discussion were based and that it provided the basis for a *revolutionary* Marxist attitude; and he said of the amendment, which was also signed by Lenin amongst others, that it alone expressed Marxist ideas clearly. G. Zinoviev, 'The Second Internationale and the Problem of War', published in *Sbornik Sotsial-demokrata*, October 1916, later included in a collection of articles of the period published by Lenin himself: V. I. Lenin and G. Zinoviev, *Gegen den Strom. Aufsätze aus den Jahren 1914–1916*, pp. 476, 477. Verlag der Kommunistischen Internationale, 1921.

160. In another article of Zinoviev's ('Once more on the subject of civil war') dated 29 February 1916, reprinted in the above mentioned collection *Gegen den Strom*, pp. 321–327, he said that Rosa Luxemburg's amendment – which she incidentally put forward on behalf of the Russian and the Polish parties – expressed the view of the Bolshevist party on civil war and that this had remained unchanged since 1907. The resolution on the position of current socialist trends passed by the First Congress of the Third Internationale also used this amendment as a point of reference to describe the Marxist trends within the Second Internationale.

161. It is proper for us to consider not the interests of some capitalist clique in wanting peace but only the resistance of the enlightened masses of the people as a factor for peace. ('Um Marokko', in *Leipziger Volkszeitung*, 14 July 1911, reprinted in *ARS II*, pp. 382, 383.)

162. We are of the opinion that wars can only be waged as long as the masses of workers either enthusiastically join in, because they

consider it a just and necessary cause, or at least patiently accept
it. When on the other hand the great majority of working people
have become convinced – and it is the task of us Social Democrats
to awaken this conviction and awareness within them – when, I
say, the majority of the people have become convinced that wars
are barbarous, deeply immoral, reactionary and against the interests
of the people, then wars will have become impossible . . . Those
who wear the so called King's uniform are but a part of the working people and when the latter have recognized how detestable and
contrary to the interests of the people wars are, then even the
soldiers will realize of their own accord without our needing to
appeal to them, what they have to do in a given case. (*Militarismus,
Krieg und Arbeiterklasse, Pol. Schr. II*, pp. 10 and 15.)

163. German social democracy obstinately refused to take seriously
the danger of war prophesied by Rosa Luxemburg and her colleagues.
At the same congress in Stuttgart, Bebel had given the assurance that
'in the influential circles of Germany, hardly anyone wants war.'
Protokoll, op. cit., p. 83. Even in 1911, in the middle of the Moroccan
crisis, when the German cruiser *Panther* had entered the port of
Agadir, a proposal by the French socialists, supported by the English
and the Spaniards, for an international demonstration against
imperialistic ventures was rejected by the executive of the German
Social Democratic Party in a letter from the secretary Molkenbuhr in
which it was said that the party must occupy itself with internal
matters and could not incur electoral risks by taking action over a
matter of international concern. When this letter was published, Rosa
Luxemburg succeeded in arousing strong indignation against the
executive but after a formal withdrawal they continued to pursue
their customary policy, cf G. Haupt, *Le Congrès manqué*, p. 34. Paris,
1965.

164. 'Krise', *Pol. Schr. II*, p. 110.

165. Absolutism in Russia must be overthrown by the proletariat. But
the proletariat needs a high degree of political education, of class
consciousness and organization in order to do this. All this cannot
be acquired from pamphlets and fly-sheets but only from the living
school of politics, through action and in action as the revolution
progresses. ('Massenstreik', *Pol. Schr. I*, pp. 158, 159.)

166. 'Bericht', *op. cit.* p. 30, note 1. In this report, Rosa Luxemburg
expressed the view that social democracy must incite the proletariat
to fight for every economic and political goal and enable it to understand the inter-relationships within society and recognize society as a
whole, thus helping it towards a mature class consciousness. So she
reminded it that the attitude of the government towards the economic
disputes (the ban on strikes and on workers' associations and defence
funds; intervention by the police and the army in labour disputes,

etc.) must force the working classes to fight in the sphere of politics as well and so make 1 May not just a struggle for an eight-hour day but also a day to demand universal suffrage, the right of association and assembly, freedom of conscience, of speech and of the press, etc.

167. In the political battle, in the long run, the mass-will cannot continue to express itself artificially in one way or be confined to one single form. It must increase and intensify, adopt fresh and more effective forms. Once kindled, mass action must march on. And if at a given moment, the leading party is too irresolute to issue the necessary watchwords, then the masses are bound to be somewhat disappointed, their enthusiasm flags and their action collapses. ('Was weiter?' in *ARS II*, pp. 325, 326.)

168. 'Ermattung oder Kampf?' in *NZ XXVIII* (1909–1910) 2, No. 35, p. 257, and No. 36.
169. 'Um Marokko', *ARS II*, p. 383.
170. 'Ermattung oder Kampf?' in *NZ*, 3 June 1910, p. 303. cf also in 'Was nun?' (*Gleichheit*, 5 February 1912, reprinted in *GW III*, p. 530.)

An offensive all along the line: in the fight for universal suffrage in Prussia, in the fight against imperialism, in the fight for cheaper bread and in positive action in social policy.

171. 'Was nun?' *op. cit. GW III*, p. 527.
172. 'Navalism' means militarism applied to the navy. In the struggle for naval supremacy launched against England by Kaiser Wilhelm II the navy played a particularly important role in German policy.
173. 'Zeit der Aussaat' in *Volkswacht*, 25 March 1910, reprinted in *ARS II*, p. 341.

174. In a party like the German one where the principle of organization and party discipline is maintained to such an unprecedented extent and where, as a result, any initiative by the unorganized masses of the people, their spontaneous, as it were improvised, capacity for action, which has been an important and often decisive factor in all previous major political struggles, are more or less impossible, then the party has an inescapable duty. . . . ('Was weiter?' *GW IV*, p. 514.)

For the powerlessness of the unorganized masses cf especially: 'Massenstreik', *Pol. Schr. I*, chapters V and VI.
175. 'Militarismus', *Pol. Schr. II*, p. 15.
176. 'Die künftige Revanche', in *Sozialdemokratische Korrespondz*, 20 January 1914, reprinted in *ARS II*, p. 484.
177. 'Geknickte Hoffnungen', *op. cit. ARS II*, pp. 181, 182.

178. The growing strength of the Russian labour movement in recent years, which is spreading through bloody demonstrations and vast strikes, offers every socialist the best possible guarantee for the

destruction of Russian despotism. The news of the revolutionary battle of the Russian proletariat was most enthusiastically received, not only by the peoples subject to the Tsar but in the whole of Europe, in both hemispheres where the banner of socialism is flying. (The article *Nacjonalism a socjaldemokracja* dates from 1903.)

179. As a result of the revolutionary events in Russia and Poland in 1905–6, at the Fourth Party Congress in Stockholm in 1906, Rosa Luxemburg's Party, the SDKPIL, proposed that it be incorporated into the Social Democratic Labour Party of Russia (SDAPR) and Rosa Luxemburg herself took part as a delegate at the Fifth Party Congress in London in 1907, where she made two important speeches; and her Polish votes enabled the Bolsheviks to achieve a majority over the Mensheviks. The speeches are reprinted in *ARS II*, p. 274 *et seq.*

180. 'Massenstreik', *Pol. Schr. I*, pp. 202, 203.

181. *ibid.* p. 203 (Italics by L. B.), cf also the article 'Die Revolution in Russland', *N.Z*, 25 January 1905, No. 18, p. 574.

> The Russian Revolution [is] a special sort of its own, precisely because it is an extremely late-comer amongst European revolutions. Russia appeared on the world revolutionary scene as the politically most backward land . . . For this reason alone, contrary to general belief, the present Russian Revolution has the most specifically proletarian class nature of all previous revolutions.

Even Marx had been of the view that the socialist revolution would only be definitively victorious when it had triumphed in England, the home of capitalism, but that it was more likely to break out in less advanced countries on the periphery of the capitalist world. And even where England was concerned he thought that revolution would break out in Ireland, the region where capitalism was weakest.

182. In *Zwei Diktaturen*, 1904, quoted by P. Frölich, *op. cit.* p. 116, Marx now wrote that the working classes must confine themselves to

> supporting the bourgeoisie in its search for power and then, in addition, to exert revolutionary pressure on the liberal and radical bourgeoisie in its desire . . . to force the upper classes of society to push the bourgeois revolution to its logical conclusion.

183. *ARS II*, pp. 300, 301.

184. No revolution ends in any other way than with this dictatorship of a single class and now all the factors are present to enable the proletariat to do the liquidating. Of course no Social Democrat deludes himself that the proletariat can retain power: if it did that it would establish its idea of class and realize socialism. At the moment, it does not yet have sufficient force because in fact the proletariat, in the narrow meaning of the word, is still socially a minority in the Russian state. ('Blankism i socjal demokracja', in

Czerwony Sztandar (Red Flag), 27 June 1906, reprinted in *WP I*, p. 490.)

185. cf 'Krise', *Pol. Schr. II*, pp. 93–95.
186. *ibid.* p. 94.
187. L. Stern, 'Die Auswirkungen der ersten russischen Revolution von 1906–1970 auf Deutschland', in *Archivalische Forschungen zur Geschichte der deutschen Arbeiterbewegung*, p. 202. Berlin, 1955, basing himself on the evening edition of the *Hamburger Nachrichten*, of 8 December 1905, states that Rosa Luxemburg made a speech at a meeting held in Hamburg in the course of which she made a sharp reply to the anarchist Erich Mühsam, who demanded recognition for the services rendered by the anarchists in Russian; she pointed out that the leadership of the Russian Revolution was entirely in the hands of the international Social Democratic Party, in the closest sympathy with German social democracy. 'It is flesh of our flesh and blood of our blood that is now fighting in Russia.'
188. 'Massenstreik', *Pol. Schr. I*, pp. 203, 204.

189. And the methods of the 1905 Russian Revolution now seemed applicable to Germany. . . . So after 1906 gradually there began to arise a certain tension between us which was kept in check by personal friendship for a while but which finally led to a break in 1910 when my friend was trying to give the fight for universal suffrage in Prussia a turn which in her opinion would lead to revolution and in mine to a crushing defeat. (Karl Kautsky, 'Rosa Luxemburg–Karl Liebknecht–Leo Jogiches. Ihre Bedeutung für Sozialdemokratie', *Eine Skizze*, p. 15.)

190. 'Und zum drittenmal', *GW III*, p. 365.
191. *ibid.*
192. 'Massenstreik', *Pol. Schr. I*, p. 207.
193. 'Programm', *Pol. Schr. II*, p. 199.
194. The Alsatian town of Zabern where there was friction between the population and the military. In blatant abuse of his authority, the CO of the regiment stationed in Zabern, Colonel von Reuter, had a few dozen of the demonstrators arrested and held in the barrack cellars overnight; and they were roughly handled. The CO was naturally found not guilty by the Strasburg court-martial on 10 January 1914. Rosenberg wrote in this connection:

In different political circumstances, the events at Zabern would have been regarded as merely an unfortunate incident. But in the highly tense political situation of 1913, the report from Zabern moved the German people very deeply. The masses felt themselves defenceless and without protection against arbitrary actions by the military aristocracy . . . On 4 December 1913, by 293 votes to 54 with 4 abstentions, the Reichstag expressed its disapproval of the government's attitude in the Zabern affair. The most important political lesson of the Zabern business was that even the cautious central leaders were carried along by a large mass movement on the part of the opposition. (*Entstehung der Weimarer Republik*, pp. 56, 57. Frankfurt am Main, 1961.)

195. A. Rosenberg, *ibid.* p. 57.
196. W. Bartel, *op. cit.* p. 109.
197. C. Zetkin, introduction to the second edition of *Rosa Luxemburg, Die Krise der Sozialdemokratie*, p. III. Berlin, 1919.
198. *ibid.* p. IV.
199. 'Vorwärts', 15 June 1914, quoted from W. Bartel, *op. cit.* p. 125.
200. Karl Kautsky, *Eine Skizze, op. cit.* p. 13.
201. Our spiritual predecessors did not speak so much of 'the workers' but a good deal more of 'the proletariat'. The proletariat consists, first, of all the wage-earning workers as the most exploited and most underprivileged class in absolute terms, but it also consists of those sections of the population who, economically, have a dual nature, such as petty bourgeois and small farmers, who inasmuch as they have proletarian interests against their exploiters and the class domination of the State might very well be brought into the orbit of social democratic agitation and can be represented in the legislative activity of the party. ('Arbeiterbewegung und Sozialdemokratie', in *Leipziger Volkszeitung*, 4 July 1902, reprinted in *GW IV*, p. 220.)

But *cf* especially 'Massenstreik', *Pol. Schr. I*, p. 198.

And when conditions in Germany have reached the degree of maturity necessary for such a period, the hitherto unorganized and most backward sections will naturally provide the most vigorous and radical elements and will not need to be dragged along. If a general strike were to break out in Germany, it will almost certainly not be the best organized sections – and definitely not the printers – but those badly organized or not organized at all, the miners, the textile workers, perhaps even the land workers who will show the greatest capacity for action.

202. E. Bernstein, 'Streik als politisches Kampfmittel', *NZ XII* (1893–1894), I, No. 22, p. 689.
203. Parvus, 'Staatsstreich und politischer Massenstreik', *NZ XIV* (1895–1896) 2, No. 33, p. 199; No. 35, p. 261; No. 36, p. 304; No. 38, p. 356; No. 39, p. 389.
204. Rosa Luxemburg, 'Und zum drittenmal das belgische Experiment', in *NZ XX* (1901–1902), 2, No. 33, p. 203.
205. F. Mehring, 'Was nun?', *NZ XX* (1902–1903) I, No. 15, p. 449.
206. R. Hilferding, 'Zur Frage des Generalstreiks', *NZ XXII* (1903–1904), I, No. 5, p. 134.
207. G. Eckstein, 'Was bedeutet der Generalstreik?', *NZ XXII* (1903–1904), No. 12, p. 357.

NOTES 161

208. K. Kautsky, 'Allerland Revolutionäres', *NZ XXII* (1903–1904), No. 18, p. 559; No. 19, p. 588; No. 20, p. 620; No. 21, p. 652; No. 22, p. 685; No. 23, p. 732.

209. An extensively documented account of these debates is to be found in Karl Kautsky, *Der politische Massenstreik*, Berlin, 1914, written, of course, from Kautsky's point of view, as well as in H. Laufenberg, *Der politische Streik*, Stuttgart, 1914. An account of the same events from Rosa Luxemburg's point of view is to be found in P. Frölich's introduction to *Rosa Luxemburg, Gesammelte Werke*, Vol IV. A comprehensive study of the problem as it appeared after the Amsterdam Congress is contained in the book by H. Roland-Holst, *Generalstreik und Sozialdemokratie*, Dresden, 1905. An overall picture of the different international views on this question was given by an investigation conducted by the French periodical *Mouvement socialiste* which published the results in their June–July–August–September number, 1904, later reprinted by H. Lagardelle in his book *La grève générale et le socialisme – Enquête internationale – Opinions et documents*, Paris, 1905.

210. If all these observations are correct, then we are forced to the conclusion that the general strike is an instrument which in certain conditions can achieve excellent results, but that the time has not yet come for it to be successfully employed [in Germany]. (Karl Kautsky, *Allerhand Revolutionäres, op. cit.* p. 737.)

211. cf Dr R. Friedeberg, *Parlamentarismus und Generalstreik*, Berlin, 1904.

212. H. Roland-Holst, *op. cit.* p. 219.

213. A report by Police Inspector Fürstenberg dated 16 June 1906 concerning the political and trade union movement in the twelfth and thirteenth parliamentary electoral district of Saxony stated:

Whereas earlier the general strike was rejected by the German Social Democratic Party, especially by almost all its leaders, in the past year a considerable number of prominent leaders of the party have supported it and a complete change in the attitude of the party towards the general strike as a means of militant action by the workers has taken place. The whole of the radical social democratic press led by the *Leipziger Volkszeitung* came out in support of the idea of a general strike. As a result they severely condemned the negative attitude of the Social Democratic Trade Union Congress held in Cologne in May which, after an address by the trade union leader Bomelburg attacking the general strike, rejected the use of the general strike by a very large majority. The *Leipziger Volkszeitung* and the influential leaders of the Leipzig Social Democratic Party were not at all in agreement with this decision of the Trade Union Congress and did not accept this resolution and referred frequently to a pamphlet published by the Dutch Social Democratic writer Roland-Holst, *Generalstreik und*

Sozialdemokratie, which explained exactly what the essence of a general or mass strike was and agitated in favour of this form of militant action. Another keen supporter of the political general strike was the social democratic agitator and author Rosa Luxemburg, at present working at *Vorwärts*, the central organ of the party, who made a speech on the subject of the general strike at a big social democratic public meeting, in which she supported it and advocated its use, particularly in the case of a possible restriction of political rights. In a series of articles dealing with the same subject in the *Leipziger Volkszeitung*, Luxemburg recommended the use of the political general strike. Other local social democratic leaders as well as others from outside advocated the idea of a general strike at a series of meetings as well as in the press, so that this subject has been on the agenda throughout the whole year. The idea of a massive withdrawal of labour in order to gain political rights or if these rights were to be restricted has already become so deeply rooted amongst the social democratic working classes that danger is to be expected from this revolutionary means. (Reported in L. Stern, *op. cit.* pp. 240, 241.)

214. Speech at the party congress at Jena, 22 September 1905, in *ARS II*, pp. 244–246.
215. *Protokoll über die Verhandlungen der Parteitags der Sozialdemokratischen Partei Deutschlands – Abgehalten zu Jena, 17 bis 23 Sept. 1905*, p. 143. Berlin, 1905.
216. H. Roland-Holst, *op. cit.* p. 218. In fact, Bebel's whole analysis was formulated in traditional terms; the general strike was only conceived as a means of removing tactical *impasses*. In addition, Bebel rejected the parallel with the Russian Revolution. cf Schorske, *op. cit.* p. 42 *et seq.*
217. P. Frölich, introduction to *R. Luxemburg, Gesammelte Werke, IV*, p. 68.
218. 'Krise', *Pol. Schr. II*, p. 133.
219. 'Massenstreik', *Pol. Schr. I*, p. 141.
220. *ibid.* p. 143.
221. Letter of 5 February 1906 to the Kautskys, in *R. Luxemburg Briefe an Karl und Luise Kautsky, 1896–1918*, p. 104. Berlin, 1923.
222. 'Massenstreik', *Pol Schr. I*, p. 164. cf also p. 198:

Six months of a period of revolution will complete the work of educating these now unorganized masses, something which ten years of popular meetings and distributing pamphlets cannot achieve.

223. 'Massenstreik', *Pol. Schr. I*, p. 189.

224. The events in Moscow give an idea, on a reduced scale, both of the logical development and of the future of the revolutionary movement as a whole; it will inevitably lead to general and open

insurrection which, however, cannot succeed except by learning from a series of partial uprisings which will prepare the way but as a result will end for the moment in what appear to be partial defeats, so that each of them may seem 'premature' considered in isolation. ('Massenstreik', *Pol. Schr. I*, p. 171.)

cf however especially 'Sozialreform', *Pol. Schr. I*, p. 122.

225. cf the passage already quoted from 'Massenstreik', *Pol. Schr.* I, p. 198, note 45.

226. 'Massenstreik', *Pol. Schr. I*, p. 193.

227. cf note 59, p. 144.

228. cf E. Schorske, *op. cit.* p. 248 *et seq.* Even left wingers like Radek and Pannekoek voted for it. cf P. Frölich, *op. cit.* pp. 211, 212.

229. In the *Notes of a Publicist* quoted at the beginning of this book (note 1, p. 137), Lenin enumerates the following 'errors' of Rosa Luxemburg: the question of the independence of Poland, her judgement on Menshevism, her theory on the accumulation of capital, the question of the unity of the Bolsheviks and the Mensheviks and finally her work written in 1918 on the Russian Revolution.

230. 'What is to be done?' *op. cit. Vol* II, p. 98.

231. So socialistic awareness is something brought into the proletariat's class struggle from outside, not something that has sprung up inside. (Karl Kautsky, 'Die Revision des Programms der Sozialdemokratie in Österreich', *NX XX* (1901–1902), p. 80.)

Kautsky's influence on Lenin's thought was presumably greater than had been commonly supposed and it would be interesting to examine their relationship. Kautsky had, alas, as we already pointed out, not absorbed Marxist dialectics; it was foreign to his way of thinking.

232. The workers begin by forming combinations against the bourgeoisie; they club together to keep up the rate of wages; they found permanent associations in order to make provision beforehand for the occasional revolts. Now and then the workers are victorious but only for a time. The real fruit of their battles lies not in the immediate result but in the ever expanding union of the workers. This union is helped by the improved means of communication created by modern industry which place workers of different localities in contact with one another. It was just this contact that was needed to centralize the numerous local struggles, all of the same character, into one national struggle between classes. But every class struggle is a political struggle. (*Manifesto of the Communist Party*, Karl Marx and Frederick Engels, Selected Works, p. 45. Lawrence and Wishart, London, 1968.)

233. . . . The *Socialists* and *Communists* are the theoreticians of the proletarian class so long as the proletariat is not yet sufficiently developed to constitute itself as a class and consequently so long as

the struggle itself of proletariat against the bourgeoisie has not yet assumed a political character . . . these theoreticians are merely Utopians, who . . . to meet the wants of the oppressed classes improvise systems and go in search of a regenerating science. But to the extent that history moves forward, and with it the struggle of the proletariat assumes clearer outlines . . . they have only to take note of what is happening before their eyes and to become its mouthpiece. (*The Poverty of Philosophy*, p. 140, London.)

cf also the introduction to the *Fragebogen für Arbeiter* (published in the *Revue Socialiste* of 20 April 1880) in which Marx, speaking of the workers, says that 'only they and no providential redeemers can produce the vigorous remedies needed for the wretched social conditions from which they are suffering.' Basically, spontaneity as understood by Rosa Luxemburg is closely related to the historical self-reliance (*geschichtiche Selbsttätigkeit*) of the working classes of which Marx speaks in his *Manifesto* and which has always remained the basis of Marxism.

234. 'The emancipation of the working classes [must] be won by the working classes themselves.' 'Provisorische Statuten der Internationalen Arbeiter–Assoziation', *Werke*, 16. p. 14.

235. 'Krise', *Pol. Schr. II*, p. 102.

236. Today in the light of Stalin's statement, it may be instructive to read once more Lenin's remarks on 'democratic centralism' which Rosa Luxemburg criticized; Lenin said that 'bureaucracy' (as opposed to democracy) was the right way to organize a revolutionary party; it emanates from the top and [favours] the further extension of the rights and authority of the central body against the party. (V. I. Lenin, *One Step Forwards, Two Steps Back*, V. I. Lenin, *Selected Works*, Vol. II, p. 409, Lawrence and Wishart.)

237. 'Organisationsfragen', *Pol. Schr. III*, p. 89.

238. 'Massenstreik', *Pol. Schr. I*, p. 199. cf also.

The task of social democracy and its leaders is not to be dragged along by events but consciously to anticipate them, survey the direction in which they are developing, shorten that development by deliberate action and hasten their course. (R. Luxemburg, *Das Offiziösentum der Theorie*, reprinted in *GW IV*, p. 669.)

239. 'Massenstreik', *Pol. Schr. I*, p. 183, cf also in 'Was weiter?' *GW IV*, p. 509:

But if the recent impressive street demonstrations reveal in themselves a welcome innovation in our methods of open militant action and at the same time have launched the mass struggle for universal suffrage in Prussia with great vigour, they impose on their part certain duties on the party whose initiative and leadership brought them about. Our party must have a clear and definite plan as to how it intends to continue the mass action which it has kindled.

240. As far as the practical application of the general strike in Germany is concerned, history will decide, just as it did in Russia; history in which social democracy and its decisions will, of course be an important factor but only one factor amongst many. ('Massenstreik', *Pol. Schr. I*, p. 145.)

To be sure, revolutions cannot be made to order. But this is also in no way the task of the Socialist Party. Its duty is only 'to say what is' at all times and fearlessly, that is to say, to show the masses clearly and plainly what they have to do at a given moment of history, to proclaim the political action programme and the watchwords arising out of the situation. Socialism must bravely leave to history itself any concern as to whether and when a mass revolutionary uprising results from this. If it fulfils its responsibilities in this way, then it can be a powerful factor in triggering off the revolutionary elements of a situation and help to hasten the outbreak of mass actions. ('Brennende Zeitfragen', in *Spartakus*, No. 6, August 1917, reprinted in *Spartakusbriefe*, p. 366. Berlin, 1958.)

241. The history of all previous revolutions teaches us that violent popular movements, far from being arbitrarily and consciously produced by so called 'leaders' or parties, are rather completely elementary social phenomena asserting their natural force and springing from the class nature of modern society. The rise of social democracy has till now done nothing to change the nature of this state of affairs nor does its role consist of laying down laws for the historical development of the class struggle but on the contrary of serving these laws and thus this development. ('Und zum dritten Male', *op. cit.* p. 275.)

The events in Frankfurt in May 1868 could be an example of Rosa Luxemburg's thesis.

242. Letter to Mathilde Wurm, 16 February 1917, in *Briefe an Freunde, op. cit.* p. 47. The expression, 'Thalassa, the eternal ocean' is taken from a poem by Heine. The rest of the letter makes it plain that Rosa Luxemburg did not rely on the spontaneity of the masses but rather considered it necessary for the political leaders to organize their tactics not in accordance with the moods of the masses but in accordance with the laws of historical development.

243. 'Programme', *Pol Schr. II*, p. 187.

244. 'Massenstreik', *Pol. Schr. I*, p. 199.

245. 'Krise', *Pol. Schr. II*, p. 21.

246. 'Organisationsfragen', *Pol. Schr. III*, p. 105.

247. This is a living transplant of the ideas of conspiracy into the labour movement, the ideas of Blanqui on the role of the masses

during revolutions, which the socialists 'invoke' when 'necessary' 'at the decisive moment', just as you bring on a 'walk-on part' when needed to complete the actors' speeches. (Letter of 4 June 1905, in Z pola walki, 1931, Nos. 11, 12.)

248. 'Organisationsfragen', in Pol. Schr. III, p. 88.
249. It is, however, interesting that in his list of Rosa Luxemburg's 'errors' in 1922 Lenin did not mention the alleged 'cult of spontaneity' on which he later so much insisted.
250. 'Organisationsfragen', in Pol. Schr. III, pp. 88, 89. cf also the speech at the Jena Party Congress, 1905, 'Protokoll', op. cit. p. 321.
251. G. Zinoviev and L. Trotsky, 'Discours', op. cit. p. 17.
252. O. K. Flechtheim, introduction to Rosa Luxemburg, Die Russische Revolution, p. 15. Frankfurt, a.M. 1963.
253. 'Massenstreik', Pol. Schr. 1, p. 220.
254. ibid. 222.
255. ibid. p. 222.
256. 'Organisationsfragen', Pol. Schr. III, p. 92.
257. cf also Liebknecht's observation on the arguments put forward by Rosa Luxemburg ('too much discipline', 'too little spontaneity') reported by E. Meyer, 'Zur Entstehungsgeschichte der Junius-Thesen', in Unter dem Banner des Marxismus, 1925, No. 2, p. 420.

258. The war broke out and comrade Luxemburg devoted her energies from the very first day to anti-war propaganda. She hoped to bring together a select band of German comrades to work together. Above all she saw the need for a manifesto signed by a number, even a small number, of personalities popular amongst the workers. Tyzka [Jogiches] decided straightaway that this would be pointless. Nevertheless we made the attempt with Rosa. But when invited to meet in her house to discuss the question, only seven people replied and only two of them – Mehring and Lensch – were eminent members of the party. The latter promised to sign but later withdrew. The manifesto would have been signed only by Luxemburg, Zetkin and Mehring, which was an impossible situation and the plan had to be dropped. (J. Marchlevski, 'Un souvenir de Rosa Luxemburg et de Jogiches', in Internationale Communiste, No. 3.)

259. For the same reason, on 4 August 1914 Liebknecht followed party discipline and voted for the military estimates, although he had spoken against them in the parliamentary party group. It was only at the second vote, on 2 December 1918, that he decided to ignore party discipline.
260. cf E. Collotti, 'Sinistra radicale & spartachisti nella social democrazia tedesca attraverso le Spartakus–Briefe', in Annali Feltrinelli, 1961, p. 16.

Reflecting the attitude which was at that time general amongst the minority, Paul Schwenk confesses that 'in our actions the

thought of splitting the party never once entered our minds', that is
to say, it was a matter of acting within the party framework, in the
expectation of changing its course by pressure from below.

261. 'During the war [I tried] to preserve the organization of the
party as long as possible, whereas Rosa preached schism.' (Karl
Kautsky, *Eine Skizze, op. cit.* p 16.) The need to break away was
incidentally also advocated in the report drawn up by Rosa Luxemburg for the group of her friends at that time called the International
Group and later the Spartakus Group. What is certain is that the
criticism of Rosa Luxemburg for not having brought about a split is
an afterthought; up to the outbreak of the World War even Lenin had
never made any such criticism.
262. 'Briefe an Freunde', *op. cit* p. 157.
263. *ibid.* p. 161. Presumably Rosa Luxemburg is alluding to Karl
Kautsky's article 'Die Aussichten der russischen Revolution', *NZ*,
6 April 1917 (XXXV, 1916–1917), 2, No. 1.
264. *cf* E. Collotti, *op. cit.* p. 66.
265. 'Die Revolution in Russland', in *Spartakus* No. 4, April 1917,
SB, p. 303.
266. 'Brennende Zeitfragen II, Die Diktatur des Proletariats', in
Spartakus, No. 6, August 1917, SB, p. 355 *et. seq.*
267. From Rosa Luxemburg's letters to Franz Mehring, in *Die Internationale*, 1 February 1917, 1923 (VI. 3), p. 69. *cf* also the letter of 24
November 1917 to Luise Kautsky in which she talks of the Russian
Revolution as a 'world historical act, whose trace will not vanish for
aeons'. *Briefe an Karl und Luise Kautsky, op. cit.* p. 192.
268. 'Zwei Osterbotschaften', in *Spartakus*, No. 5, May 1917, SB, p.
350.
269. *cf* also E. Collotti, *op. cit.* p. 70.
270. Arthur Rosenberg writes:

The deaths of Rosa Luxemburg and Liebknecht were an extremely grave loss for the socialist labour movement because both
persons represented a scientifically based socialism, taking account
of actual conditions and thus consistent . . . But above all, as
leaders of the German Communist Party, Rosa Luxemburg and
Karl Liebknecht would never have allowed themselves to be mis-
used as tools of Russian State policy. They would have possessed
sufficient authority to guard against so-called Leninism after 1921.
The fatal development which made Germany's specific brand of
socialism the liege of Russian peasant policies and thereby crippled
it would perhaps have been avoided had they both lived longer.
(*Geschichte der Weirmarer Republik*, p. 62.)

Undoubtedly with the deaths of the group of German leaders (Luxemburg, Liebknecht, Mehring and Jogiches), but above all that of Rosa
Luxemburg, there disappeared the only people who would have been

able to talk with Lenin and the other Bolshevist leaders on equal terms.

271. This is an unfinished manuscript on the Russian Revolution written during her last few weeks in prison and perhaps not intended for publication by her. It was published by Paul Levi under the title *Die russische Revolution. Eine kritische Würdigung. Aus dem Nachlass von Rosa Luxemburg, herausgegeben und eingeleitet von Paul Levi.* Berlin, 1922.

272. G. Lukács, *Kritische Bemerkungen über Rosa Luxemburg's Kritik der russischen Revolution*, in op. cit. p. 278.

273. *Bericht an den III Internationalen Sozialistischen Arbeiterkongress in Zürich 1893 über den Stand und Verlauf der sozialdemokratischen Bewegung in Russisch-Polen 1889–1893 erstattet von der Redaktion der Zeitschrift Sprawa Robotnicza* (The Organ of the Social Democrats of the Kingdom of Poland).

274. Rosa Luxemburg, *Die industrielle Entwicklung Polens, Inaugural-Dissertation zur Erlangung der hohen Staatswissenschaftlichen Fakultät*, Zürich, Leipzig, 1898.

275. This same Rosa Luxemburg, however, wrote in her commentary on the programme of her party:

> Since our country has a certain special unity within the Russian State which distinguishes it culturally and to some extent socially and economically from the rest of the State, the Social Democratic Party of the Kingdom of Poland demands, in addition to general legal equality for all nationalities, self-government for the country, that is to say, autonomy for Poland. This means that she wishes all problems concerning our country to be solved by our own officials and our own Parliament, elected by all adult citizens of the country by equal, universal, secret and direct ballot and further that Polish schools, law courts and other indispensable institutions be organized by us and subject to Parliament. (*Czego chcemy? Komentarz do programu socjaldemokracji Kroletswa Polskiego i Litwy* ('What do we want? Commentary on the programme of the SDKIL'), p. 67. Warsaw, 1906.)

276. All this could have been guaranteed by Germany while still preserving her interests and honour if she had had the courage after the Revolution, in her own interests, to demand weapons in hand, that Russia should give up Poland . . . The only possible, the only solution which would have preserved Germany's interests, we repeat, was war with Russia.

These words were written by Marx on 20 August 1848, in an article for the *Neue Rheinische Zeitung*, commenting on the debates on the Polish question in the Frankfurt Assembly. For Marx's attitude towards the Polish question in 1848, see F. Mehring's detailed introduction, 'Die polnische Frage' in *Aus dem literarischen Nachlass von*

Karl Marx, Friedrich Engels und Ferdinand Lassalle, herausgegeben von F. Mehring, III, pp. 18–44. Stuttgart, 1902.
For the role of the Polish question in Marx's strategy, cf also Engel's letter of 23 May 1951 to Marx:

> The more I think about history, the clearer it seems to me that the Poles are *une nation foutue,* who can only be used as a means until Russia herself is dragged into the agrarian revolution.

cf also Marx's first published manuscripts on Poland in K. Marx, *Manuskripte über die polnische Frage (1863–1864), herausgegeben und eingeleitet von W. Conze and D. Hertz-Eichenrode.* The Hague, 1961.
277. cf Marx's letter of 18 August 1869 to Engels:

> In Poznan . . . the Polish workers (joiners, etc.) have brought a strike* to a victorious conclusion by the help of their Berlin colleagues. This struggle against *Monsieur le Capital* – even in the subordinate form of a strike* – is a very different way of getting rid of national prejudices from that of the bourgeois gentlemen with their peace declarations. (*Marx-Engels Correspondence 1864–1895,* a selection with a commentary and notes, p. 263. London, 1934.)

278. cf to some extent the open letter of Daszynski, the greatest leader of the party published in the party organ *Naprzod* (Forwards) in December 1905 and Rosa Luxemburg's replies in *Czerwony Sztandar* (Red Flag).
279. cf Nettl, *op. cit.* p. 853 and in this connection the whole of the interesting *Appendix* 2 in Nettl's book which gives extensive information about the different aspects of the controversy. Also to be recommended are some recent Polish studies, all in *Z pola walki,* such as W. Najdus, *Z historu ksztaltowania sie pogladów SDKiL w kwestii narodnowej,* No. 3 (19), 1962, p. 31. J. Kanccwiz, *Rewolucja spoleczna, kwestia narodowa i SDKiL,* No. 1 (29), 1965, p. 65, also E. Kuszko, *Tadycje ruchu robotniczego a westia narodawa,* No. 4 (32), 1965, p. 87; W. Konderski, *U zródepogladów SDKiL na kwestie narodawa,* No. 2 (38), 1967, p. 83; W. Najdus, *Poglody grup SDKiL i KPRP w Rosji w latach 1917–1920 no kwestie narodawa, ibid.* p. 114.
280. V. I. Lenin. On the right of nations to self-determination in: *Selected Works,* Vol. 4, p. 252. Lawrence and Wishart, London, 1936.
281. V. I. Lenin, *ibid.* pp. 252, 256.
282. Preface to *Die polnische Frage und die sozialistische Bewegung.* From the Italian translation by L. Basso, *Rosa Luxemburg, Scritti politici,* p. 267. Rome, 1967.
283. Here is an apt example:

> For the socialists, the indubitable right of every nation to independence was and is clear, for this, too, proceeds from the basic principles of socialism (*ibid.* pp. 261–262.)

* In English in the text.

Once again in this article from which we have already quoted so much, Lenin is saying that it is merely a matter of recognizing this right:

> For this reason, the proletariat confines itself to the, as it were, negative demand for the *right* to self-determination, without even guaranteeing it to any single nation and without committing itself to give *anything at all* at the expense of any other nation. (Lenin, *op. cit.* p. 264.)

Further on he explains that it is the same attitude which the socialists adopted to divorce, where the right of divorce does not mean that it actually wants to loosen the bands of marriage. As we saw, Rosa Luxemburg was not fighting against the general right of self-determination but against the specific slogan of fighting for Poland's independence which was being preached to the Polish proletariat.

284. Preface, *op. cit.* p. 271.

285. The programme of the Russian Social Democrats expressly stated that the party would support every revolutionary or opposition movement against the existing regime in Russia. And Lenin declared:

> The Social Democrats [provide] this support in order to hasten the overthrow of the common enemy . . . The Social Democrats support every revolutionary movement directed against the present social order, every oppressed nationality, every persecuted religion, every enslaved class, etc. (V. I. Lenin, *The Tasks of Russian Social Democrats, op. cit.* Vol 1, p. 502.)

286. V. I. Lenin, *The Discussion on Self-Determination Summed Up. Collected Works*, Vol 22, pp. 347, 348. Lawrence and Wishart, London.

287. As we have already repeatedly emphasized, Rosa Luxemburg was never willing to treat the subject in isolation. In an article for the Fourth Party Congress of the SDKIL, published in the official periodical *Przeglad Socjaldemokratyczny* in August 1903, she pointed out that the slogan of solidarity of the Polish proletariat with that of Russia, as opposed to the social patriotic slogans, was,

> at the moment when the Social Democrats came on the scene, an urgent political necessity and not the expression of an abstract idea based on the principles of scientific socialism. It was the moment when social patriotism was putting forward its programme for the re-establishment of Poland for the first time [May 1893] and through its chauvinistic agitation was at the same time trying to isolate socialism in Poland from the movement in Russia, indeed to base Polish socialism on the conflicting political interests and trends of the Polish and Russian working classes. ('IV Zjasd Socjaldemokrasji KPiL', in *Przeglad Socjaldemokratyczny*, No. 8, 1903. [Italian trans-

lation in L. Basso, introduction to *R. Luxemburg, Scritti politici*, p. 118, note 26.])

288. cf Rosa Luxemburg's observations on the role of nationalism in its attempt to harness the socialist parties to the equivalent national bourgeois carts, in her fragment of an article 'Krieg, nationale Frage und Revolution', published by F. Weil in *Archiv für die Geschichte des Sozialmus und der Arbeiterbewegung*, 1928, p. 292 *et seq.*, reprinted in *Pol. Schr. III*, p. 142 *et seq.*

289. A. Warski, 'Rosa Luxemburgs Stellung zu den taktischen Problemen der Revolution', 1922, p. 7, quoted in P. Frölich, *op. cit.* p. 298.

290. 'Russische Revolution', *Pol. Schr. III*, p. 116.

291. cf the article 'Die Nationalversammlung', in *Rote Fahne*, 20 November 1918, reprinted in *ARS II*, p. 606.

292. 'Russische Revolution', *Pol. Schr. III*, p. 139.

293. *ibid.* pp. 134, 136.

294. *ibid.* p. 136.

295. On this question cf L. Basso, 'Da Stalin a Krusciov', *op. cit.*

296. 'Russische Revolution', *Pol. Schr. III*, p. 140.

297. Similarly the class nature of the political organ that has to realize the present proletarian revolution, that is to say, the workers' parliament, the body representing the town and country proletariats, is a symbol of the new social order of society for which this revolution stands, a symbol, too, of the class nature of its specific task. The National Assembly is an outdated legacy of bourgeois illusions of 'one united people', of the liberty, equality and fraternity of the bourgeois State. Anyone who has recourse to a National Assembly today is merely, whether consciously or not, turning the clock back to the historical stage of bourgeois revolution; he is either a secret agent of the bourgeoisie or an unconscious upholder of the petit bourgeoisie. ('Die Nationalversammlung', *ARS II*, pp. 605, 606.)

National Assembly or government by the councils? That is the second item on the agenda of the Reich Assembly of the Workers' and Soldiers' Councils and it poses the central question of the revolution at this moment. Either a National Assembly or else the whole power to go to the workers' and soldiers' councils; either abandoning socialism or launching the sharpest possible class struggle against the bourgeoisie with every weapon available to the proletariat: – that is the dilemma. What an idyllic plan to realize socialism by parliamentary methods, by a simple decision of the majority. What a pity that this cloud cuckoo dream takes no account whatsoever of the historical experience of bourgeois revolution, not to mention the specific nature of the proletarian revolution. ('Nationalversammlung oder Räteregiering?' in *Rote Fahne*, 17 December 1918, reprinted in *ARS II*, p. 640.)

298. In the Spartakus programme, written in the heat of the German Revolution, Rosa Luxemburg said:

This whole resistance must be broken step by step, with an iron hand and relentless energy. The force of the bourgeois counter-revolution must be met by the revolutionary force of the proletariat. ('Was will der Spartakusbund?', pamphlet (1918), reprinted in *Pol. Schr. II*, p. 164.)

299. 'Russische Revolution', *Pol. Schr. III*, pp. 140, 141.
300. *ibid.* p. 108.
301. Radek, her companion in arms in many a struggle, wrote:

The fact that Rosa Luxemburg was as deeply rooted in the Polish and Russian as in the German labour movements and that with her intimate knowledge of the history of the international labour movement she was at home in the problems of both French and English socialism, made her the representative of the internationalism of the Communist movement and her loss is not only the loss of the leader of German Communism but also that of the most eminent mouthpiece of the international nature of our movement. (*op cit.* p. 25.)

At the end of his biography to which I have already frequently referred, J. P. Nettl devotes several pages to her 'extreme and dogmatic internationalism' (Appendix 2, *Die nationale Frage*) and concludes with the statement that

to a greater extent than any other Marxist, she transferred to the working classes the feelings of loyalty normally reserved for one's country. More than anyone else, Rosa Luxemburg was concerned to put Marx's concept of class in the centre of the system of relationships in society and break down the old limits of nationality. In this respect her contribution remains unsurpassed. (J. P. Nettl, *op. cit.* p. 829.)

302. 'I feel at home anywhere in the world where there are clouds and birds and human tears' she wrote in a letter of 16 February 1917 to Mathilde Wurm from prison. (*Briefe an Freunde*, p. 49.) Radek (*op. cit.* p. 26) speaks of this great humanity of Rosa Luxemburg which appealed to everyone who was in contact with her and H. Roland-Holst (*op. cit.* pp. 41, 42) speaks of

the elemental feeling of solidarity which penetrated her being to the point of identification – links with animals, plants and mankind, with all life that was suffering but also joyful and conscious of its joy.

303. cf the article, attributed to Mehring, 'Die Parteinahme der deutschen Sozialdemokratie für den Krieg', published in *Nieder-*

barnimer Referentenmaterial, reprinted in *SB* p. 5 *et seq.* in which the author condemned the way in which

the whole organized power of the German Social Democratic Party and of the trade unions was put at the service of the government which was waging war and used to stifle revolutionary energy.

cf also E. Collotti, *Sinistra radicale e Spartachisti, op. cit.* pp. 16, 17. 304. *Briefe au Freunde*, p. 157.
305. 'Zwei Osterbotschaften', in *Spartakus*, No. 11, reprinted in *SB* p. 460.
306. 'Die geschichtliche Verantwortung', in *Spartakus*, No. 8, reprinted in *SB* p. 409.
307. 'Die russische Tragödie', in *Spartakus*, No. 11, reprinted in *SB* p. 460.
308. The abolition of the domination of capital, the realization of a socialistic order of society, this and nothing less than this is the historical theme of the present revolution. ('Der Anfang' in *Die Rote Fahne*, 18 April 1918, reprinted in *ARS LL*, p. 594.)
309. The Independent Socialdemocratic Party of Germany had been founded at the Gotha Party Conference (5–8 April 1917) by the socialists who disagreed with the war policy of the party and had already been outlawed by the leading party organs. The right wing of the new party was represented by Kautsky and Bernstein, the extreme left by the Spartakists, who only remained in the party after hesitation and internal dispute and preserved their autonomy as a group. In the middle there were people like Haase and Ledebour. The party's line was not a revolutionary one but rather inclined to the centre; but the Berlin workers and their leaders who were fighting under the Independent flag adopted a revolutionary attitude.
310. On the struggle for power at this time in Germany cf H. E. Friedländer's article on the subject, 'Conflict of Revolutionary Authority: Provisional Government vs. Berlin Soviet, Nov.-Dec. 1918', in *International Review of Social History*, 1962, No. 2, p. 163 *et seq.*
311. cf particularly the articles 'Die Nationalversammlung' and 'Nationalversammlung oder Räteregierung?', in the *Rote Fahne* of 20 November and 17 December 1918, reprinted in *ARS II*, pp. 603 and 640. Her main argument was that the National Assembly would mean a strengthening of the power of the bourgeoisie whereas the needs of a socialist revolution required power to be in the hands of the workers through organizations that were the expression of their class.
312. As Nettl (*op. cit.* p. 712) rightly points out, Rosa Luxemburg's idea of democracy is not to be confused with the formal idea of democracy in the sense that you should first have a majority and then proceed to act. She believed rather in the power of action to create awareness, so that the majority would arise out of the revolutionary struggle. For this reason the seizure of power was the

conclusion of a process, the first stage of which was the revolutionary struggle of a minority and the second, the establishment of a majority by means of this struggle.

313. 'Was will der Spartakusbund?', *Pol. Schr. II*, p. 162.

314. *ibid.* p. 164.

315. *Briefe an Freunde*, p. 173.

316. W. Pieck, 'The Founding of the Communist Party in Germany', in *International Press Correspondence IX* (1929), No. 1.

317. P. Frölich, *op. cit.* pp. 336, 338.

318. In her book *Um Rosa Luxemburg's Stellung zur russischen Revolution*, p. 83 *et seq. Verlag der Kommunistischen Internationale,* 1922, Clara Zetkin describes the difficult position of Rosa Luxemburg and Leo Jogiches as opponents of the insurrection and its slogans: as a result on the one hand they found themselves forced to express their own opinions plainly and on the other hand they felt it their duty not to leave the masses in the lurch in their struggle and so were torn between a negative critical attitude and a positive progressive one.

319. Liebknecht and Rosa Luxemburg would have had no difficulty in leaving Berlin in good time and seeking safety somewhere in Germany. But out of a mistaken conception of honour, they refused to 'flee' and so they remained in Berlin, although the whole hatred of the bourgeoisie and of the officers was concentrated on the two main Spartakist 'trouble makers'. The great revolutionaries of the past knew what they meant for the movement as persons. They were never afraid to abandon their homes when the interests of the cause required it. Marx and Engels did not scruple to go to England in 1849 and they would not have dreamt of placing themselves at the disposal of the legal processes of the German counterrevolution. In the summer of 1917 Lenin left Petersburg in order to escape pursuit by Kerensky's government. He went underground in Finland and only returned to Petersburg when it was no longer foolhardy to do so. Rosa Luxemburg was a woman of genius and the best theoretical mind in the German labour movement but she still retained certain traces of a petty bourgeois 'sense of decency'. This is how I interpret her submission to the majority of her colleagues, her collaboration in the stupid uprising in January, where she also wanted to show loyalty to the others, and finally her refusal to flee which cost her her life. (A. Rosenberg, *op. cit.* p. 61.)

Max Adler saw her as

perhaps making this mistake deliberately, springing with desperate courage into the breach caused by social-patriotism and the flagging revolutionary spirit of socialism and trying to fill it with all the wild self-sacrificing devotion of her revolutionary will to fight. (Max Adler, 'Karl Liebknecht und Rosa Luxemburg', in *Der Kampf,* February 1919, p. 84.)

320. It is a sign of the unity of theory and practice in Rosa Luxemburg's life's work that this unity of victory and defeat, of individual destiny and global process formed the main thread of her theory and her way of life. . . . The fact that she stayed with the masses and shared their fate when she had clearly foreseen the defeat of the January uprising years before in theory and, practically, at the moment it took place, is as much the logical result of the unity of theory and practice in her actions as is the deadly hatred felt towards her and deservedly so by her assassins, the social democratic opportunists. (G. Lukács, op. cit. p. 56.)

321. This is the wording given by C. Zetkin op. cit. p. 83. A slightly different form of words is to be found in G. Zinoviev, 'Leo Tyska', in Die Kommunistische Internationale, 1919, No. 5.

322. H. Roland-Holst, op. cit. p. 88.

323. In his article quoted above, Max Adler writes (p. 75) that Rosa Luxemburg's hardest struggle was against the pitiful ignorance and abject state in which majority socialism kept the masses:

this petty self satisfaction in day-to-day successes, this complacent lack of idealism in trying to achieve power in the State whilst leaving the system of class domination completely unchanged, this trimming your sails to the wind – in a word . . . this mortification of the spirit of the class struggle in the slough of bourgeois ways of thought and feeling . . . this mortification with all its despair and desolation.

The accusation that the socialist parties were responsible for the defeats of the proletariat and even for the mistakes of the Bolsheviks runs through all her writings. cf also the epigraph to this chapter, which is taken from one of her manuscripts published several years after her death and now reprinted under the title 'Fragmente über Kriege, nationale Frage und Revolution', in Pol. Schr. III, p. 149.

324. Rosa Luxemburg's attitude to the question of the land workers deserves a separate examination which we cannot undertake in this note. In principle, we may say that she clearly saw the contradictory nature of the peasantry as being a force which was simultaneously revolutionary vis-à-vis present society but also conservative and reactionary; in practice, however, she concerned herself very little with the question because she felt much more attracted to agitating amongst the working class masses.

325. K. Kautsky, Eine Skizze, p. 20.

326. G. Lukács, op. cit. p. 281.

Index

Index